A PSYCHOANALYST ON THE COUCH

SUNY series in Contemporary French Thought

David Pettigrew and François Raffoul, editors

A PSYCHOANALYST
ON THE COUCH

JUAN-DAVID NASIO

TRANSLATED BY
STEPHANIE GRACE SCHULL

REVISED AND EDITED BY
FRANÇOIS RAFFOUL AND DAVID PETTIGREW

STATE UNIVERSITY OF NEW YORK PRESS

Juan-David Nasio, Un psychanalyste sur le divan © 2002 Editions Payot & Rivages

Published by
STATE UNIVERSITY OF NEW YORK PRESS, ALBANY

For information, contact
State University of New York Press, Albany, NY
www.sunypress.edu

Production, Eileen Meehan
Marketing, Anne M. Valentine

Library of Congress Cataloging-in-Publication Data

Nasio, Juan-David.
  [Psychanalyste sur le divan. English]
  A psychoanalyst on the couch / Juan-David Nasio ; translated by Stephanie Grace Schull ; revised and edited by François Raffoul and David Pettigrew.
    p. cm. (SUNY series in contemporary French thought)
  Includes index.
  ISBN 978-1-4384-4347-8 (hardcover : alk. paper)
  ISBN 978-1-4384-4346-1 (paperback : alk. paper)
  1. Nasio, Juan-David—Interviews. 2. Psychoanalysts—Interviews. I. Pettigrew, David, 1951– II. Raffoul, François, 1960– III. Title.

RC506.N357 2012
616.89'17—dc23   2011038840
                    10 9 8 7 6 5 4 3 2 1

The idea of this book came to me through a series of interviews with Xavier Diaz, a young psychology student. I want to thank him for the quality of his questions, for they have helped me reflect on my work, my beliefs, my doubts, and my life as a psychoanalyst. I wrote these pages in the same spirit as our dialogue.

J.-D. N.

CONTENTS

ACKNOWLEDGMENTS

I owe much to the editors of this series, David Pettigrew and François Raffoul. Not only did they review the translation and make improvements, but they long ago introduced me to Juan-David Nasio's work and to Dr. Nasio himself. I am many times indebted to them for this.

I also had the good fortune of working with Dr. Nasio in Paris under the auspices of a Chateaubriand Fellowship awarded to me by the Embassy of France. Dr. Nasio graciously accepted a curious graduate student from New York and generously gave of his time and expertise. It was a pivotal time in my doctoral studies and it was an honor and an inspiration to study with a master of the craft. I thank the French Embassy for supporting this work.

As Dr. Nasio writes in this book of having worked with Jacques Lacan when Dr. Nasio was a young foreign student on a scholarship, I likewise studied with Dr. Nasio. He welcomed me to meet with him in his office (the same office that he describes in the book) and to attend his classes at Jussieu. During our meetings I would record our conversations as part of my research, and it was a nice symmetry for me to see this book capturing the conversation between the doctor and a student. I thank Dr. Nasio for sharing his ideas in person and in writing.

Looking back, many things came together that made this translation possible. We can trace it to Freud and to Freud's predecessors, but it recently started with Jacques Lacan, then Juan-David Nasio, then Drs. Pettigrew and Raffoul, then passing through me, and now to you, the reader.

EDITORS' PREFATORY NOTE

TO THE AMERICAN EDITION

[T]he psychoanalyst is the narrator *of the unconscious.*

—J.-D. Nasio

Dr. J.-D. Nasio is the author of twenty books on psychoanalysis that have been translated into twelve languages. He was trained in the Freudian tradition and was under the formal supervision of Jacques Lacan from 1973 to 1979. In 1999, Dr. Nasio was one of the first psychoanalysts inducted into the prestigious French *Légion d'Honneur.* He is director as well of the *Séminaires Psychanalytiques de Paris.* The present book, *A Psychoanalyst on the Couch,* offers a refreshingly candid and informative account of the thinking and the practice of one of Europe's leading psychoanalysts.[1] The book is formed from a series of dialogues that Dr. Nasio had with Xavier Diaz, who was a psychology student at the time. The dialogical style as well as the nature of the questions make the discussion especially accessible to the reader, providing a unique insight into Dr. Nasio's work and his experience in psychoanalysis for the past forty years.

Early on in the book, Dr. Nasio sets forth what he sees as the fundamental responsibility of the psychoanalyst, namely the task of freeing his patients from their suffering:

> In order to liberate the patient from his or her suffering, it is necessary to understand it, and in order to understand it, it is necessary to experience it without being affected by it. To be precise, it is not the feeling of the actual suffering that brings the patient to therapy, but the older, original pain of their childhood trauma: *analysts must feel within themselves what the patients have forgotten.* (PC, 3)

Dr. Nasio explains further that working with patients is a delicate exercise, consisting in the therapist reliving the patient's forgotten emotions, and reflecting them back to him or her. As Dr. Nasio writes, in every person who suffers, there is a child who searches in vain to speak of his or her suffering: "It is precisely this suffering, powerless child, on the verge of finding the right words, who I try to imagine" (PC, 4).

In the course of the discussions with Mr. Diaz, Dr. Nasio unfolds his interpretations of a number of Freudian and Lacanian concepts that emerge in the context of his work, and rethinks them anew. These include the death drive (PC, 45), foreclosure (PC, 10), *jouissance* (PC, 81), *objet petit a* (PC, 76), psychosis (PC, 9–11), the "*Sujet-supposé-Savoir* [Subject-supposed-to-Know]" (PC, 17), and the transference (PC, 20–22). Further, in the inventive style that has come to distinguish his writings, Nasio advances a number of bold hypotheses in this book. He returns, for example, to his notion that the unconscious is an eventful phenomenon that is activated in analysis. The unconscious, he writes, "appears only at privileged moments, for example, in treatment when singular events occur, I mean when the psychoanalyst or the patient feels an intense emotion and lets out a word or a gesture that surprises him or her. The unconscious is, as such, an eventful unconscious. That is to say, there is no unconscious before or after, but only during an event; the unconscious is intrinsic to the event. This implies, and this is the second characteristic: the unconscious is never already there, at the ready, preexisting the act; but rather, it is intrinsic to the act" (PC, 79). Nasio also insists that the unconscious is something that is shared between the analyst and the patient. The unconscious is not an individual psyche, but is shared in common between partners in psychoanalysis. There is therefore not an unconscious proper to the psychoanalyst and another proper to the patient, "but one *singular and unique* unconscious produced during a surprising event in a session, the incarnation of the *in-between* of the analytic encounter" (PC, 80).

In addition to his recasting of psychoanalytical concepts, Nasio also engages metapsychological as well as cultural issues. He identifies, for instance, aspects of what he sees as a generalized social malaise, and analyzes the loss of the defining features of masculinity and the decline in paternal authority. In the course of the book, Nasio provides insights into issues of human sexuality that he has encountered as an analyst. He proposes for instance that all women participate in a fantasm of virginity. Such a fantasmatic virginity means that no one has ever "reached the profound depths of their being" (PC, 39). Nasio advances this provocative notion as a "psychoanalytic hypothesis that remains to be verified" (PC, 40). He also addresses issues in relationships, such as jealousy, humiliation, the dependency of love, love in the couple, hatred and solitude, impotency, and abandonment. At the same time, he elaborates on the positive aspects of genuine friendship and enduring love.

In addition to his writings, his teaching, his seminars, and his work with adults, Dr. Nasio is well known for his work with children. In this book, he discusses ways of communicating effectively with children. He addresses the "physiological, psychological, and social development of a child," specifying seven crises that every child experiences, along with explanatory diagrams. He details his experiences of psychoanalysis with children, dwelling on the crucial importance of the first meeting.

The interview format of the book yields personal reflections by Nasio on a number of topics. He shares his memories, for example, of his father's influence (his father was a medical doctor in Argentina, a distinguished gastroenterologist). He reflects on his arrival in France, his immersion in French culture, and his memory of his first encounter with Lacan in Paris. Nasio spent six years under Lacan's supervision, and reminisces about the day when Lacan invited him to present a lecture for his seminar. Dr. Nasio reflects as well on the extent to which he continues to be guided and inspired by Freud. Indeed, Dr. Nasio asserts that in his work he carries on what he has inherited from Freud and Lacan. Yet, he insists that this inheritance is in no way passive, in no way a matter of simple repetition, but is an effort of intensive study and reinvention. "My motto could be written: *Say well what has already been said and you will be surprised to have said something new*" (PC, 83).

—David Pettigrew and François Raffoul

HOW DOES A PSYCHOANALYST WORK?

DIVING "THE BIG BLUE"

Xavier Diaz: Before we get started, I would like to ask that you respond to my questions openly and freely, as if you were speaking to me from the psychoanalyst's couch.

J.-D. Nasio: How amusing to find myself on the couch after all these years! I am happy to play along, and I am curious to know where this will take us. In any case, working with patients is another way of my being on the couch. Why? A psychoanalyst works with expertise gained from experience and theoretical knowledge, but also with the ability to feel, fantasize, and to listen to his or her unconscious. At heart, being a psychoanalyst is to have never left the couch.

I'm glad you brought that up, as my first question has to do with the couch. Why do psychoanalysts ask their patients to lie down? The couch serves a double function for both the patient and the psychoanalyst in turn. It puts the patient at ease, allowing memories, images, sentiments, and sensations to surface more readily. When a patient reclines, his or her view of him or herself in the world changes. The patient trades an external point of view for one that's markedly internal and dream-like. With the patient reclined on the couch, the psychoanalyst is freed from having his facial expressions constantly scrutinized. To always be on guard inhibits the psychoanalyst's ability to experience the sensations and the effects of the patient's word choices on the unconscious. To ask the patient to recline is not just a simple ritual; rather, it is an essential technique that encourages intimacy in speech and facilitates careful listening.

I have a story I would like to share about the couch that I use in my practice, which I designed myself. The furniture maker recommended a small leather sofa that was very pleasing, but I thought the headboard too high. I submitted a draft of a couch with a lower headrest so that it would be even with my chair. I wanted to keep from having the appearance of being elevated or otherwise separated from the patient. It is a beautiful piece of furniture, without being ostentatious, and is most likely one of a kind. Many a time I thought of changing it, but here it is, thirty years later! On the wall above the couch is a reproduction of a painting by Brueghel. My patients often remark that it is as if the couch is divided. On the left side is the dark and monastic perspective of the Brueghel on an otherwise empty wall. On the other, there is the part of the room that is more light-filled and open.

Is the design of the office really so important?
It is crucial. I attach great value to the aesthetics of the place where I receive patients. You can sense the warmth of the office in its yellow and orange hues that make the space appear lighter and almost transparent. That is what I love about it. Some of my colleagues prefer an austere room that is somber and filled with books. Each psychoanalyst should create a space that works best for him or her and supports the work.

And how do you like to work?
I try to be close to my patients, both literally and figuratively. When the patient is in front of me, I usually sit down at the edge of my seat in order to be even more involved. If he or she is reclined, I slide the chair close to the couch to reinforce the intimacy of listening. Contrary to the caricature of the silent psychoanalyst, being distant and passive, I see the psychoanalyst as a full and active presence, completely focused on the person. As I see it, the practitioner must be a very careful observer, attentive not only to the words and the pauses of the patient, but also to his or her gestures. In fact, good listening begins with good observation. From the moment I welcome the patient in my waiting room, all of my senses, visual, auditory, olfactory, and even tactile, are awake. For example, when I greet with a handshake, I may find the hand to be cold, flaccid, or sweaty. Similarly, I pay particular attention to the packages and objects the patient may bring with him or her. I may smell the alcohol on his or her breath in spite of the mint chewing gum. Whether it is a child sitting at the game table or an adult in front of me, I remain attentive to the expressions of distraction or subtle messages in the

eyes. In short, a psychoanalyst does not only listen with the ears, he or she is receptive to all signs of body language by which thoughts are communicated.

Nevertheless, focusing our senses on the appearance of the patient is not sufficient in itself to allow us to understand and relieve their suffering. It is also necessary for us to experience this suffering, to actually relive it with the patient, but without being overwhelmed by it. It is the only way for the therapist to really understand the pain and know how to treat it effectively. One should not allow oneself to be taken over by a wave of emotion or succumb to one's compassion. That would be an obstacle to understanding the situation. Over the years, the psychoanalyst learns how to master his or her empathy and not allow it to be destabilizing. Certainly, the psychoanalyst remains human and kind, but never compassionately indulgent.

But why not be compassionate?

Because the patient does not ask for pity. The patient asks that we help him or her understand his or her anxiety and help him or her be rid of it. If we give in to compassion, we place ourselves far from the state of attention and lucidity necessary for discovering the root of their problems. We have to choose: either we are compassionate and share the pain as friends do, or while remaining sympathetic we focus our efforts on discovering, behind the patient's symptoms, the real cause of their illness. The cause is most often an emotional trauma from their childhood.

In order to liberate the patient from his or her suffering, it is necessary to understand it, and in order to understand it, it is necessary to experience it without being affected by it. To be precise, it is not the feeling of the actual suffering that brings the patient to therapy, but the older, original pain of their childhood trauma: *analysts must feel within themselves what the patients have forgotten.* Our main challenge as psychoanalysts is to succeed at this mental feat. We must feel the effects in ourselves of their earliest painful emotional experiences, which they have forgotten, while not letting ourselves be affected by it. We must represent the scene with characters who would experience the same emotions, and help the patient re-experience the intensity of that scene, by describing it with words that will carry the most meaning for them. This is a delicate exercise in psychoanalytic perception that leads the therapist to relive in him or herself the patient's forgotten emotions, and to then transmit them back to him or her. I am convinced that in order to better understand a patient we can only know them within ourselves, at our deepest depths.

Let me be even more concrete. After several months of analysis, at a critical moment in a session, I hear the patient express his or her depression. I try hard to imagine the patient as a child or as an adolescent in a conflict that was important for his or her history. *You should know that every person who suffers harbors a helpless, hurt, child, who seeks in vain to express his or her suffering.* It is precisely this suffering, powerless child, on the verge of finding the right words, who I try to imagine. I feel the effect of not the adult before me, but rather, the effect of the little boy or little girl of the childhood drama that I revive. If, during treatment, the imagined scene is confirmed to be not a simple invention on my part, I try to communicate it to the patient, thereby relieving some of the patient's suffering. Then I would believe that I had cleared up at last one of the major conflicts causing the symptoms.

Lea[1] was a young woman who came to me for a consultation about a serious phobia of streets and public places that kept her cloistered in her apartment. She left her apartment as little as possible, and was always accompanied by a friend or relative in order to come to my office for appointments. After a year of analysis, there were several decisive moments, one of which brought us to the core of her phobia. While she was crying and recounting the acts of a treacherous best friend, I recalled a dramatic scene of her childhood. When she was five years old, her father woke her up to tell her, without affect, of the inexplicable departure of her mother for a distant country. A year later, the patient learned that in reality her mother had died in an automobile accident. Lea had already told me about this horrific event in a tone that was detached and cold, as if she was indifferent. But, it was while listening to her complain of being abandoned by her friend that made me visualize the scene of another abandonment, that of her mother.

Recalling this event, I felt that I could relive the feelings of a little girl struck down by the inept announcement by her father, who was in turn overwhelmed with grief. I had felt with complete lucidity, in the moment of the session, that which Lea would have felt, albeit vaguely or confusedly, those twenty years earlier: a horrible feeling of abandonment and an icy solitude. With infinite tact,

I described the traumatic scene to her and evoked the distress that had devastated her. After my intervention, Lea was overwhelmed, as if she was reliving the confusion of the separation of which she had repressed the pain. In the month that followed the session of reawakening, we had the satisfaction of seeing the majority of her phobic anxiety gradually disappear.

I would like to share something concerning phobia that I see often in patients: when working with a phobic patient, it is always necessary to ask oneself, "Which trauma, which violent separation, which loss (or more precisely), which abandonment—real or imaginary—happened between three and six years of age, on the part of one or the other parent?" In effect, we know that the phobic fear is an anxiety provoked by the early, brutal, unspoken, loss of a loved one. I emphasize that this loss could take place objectively in reality or subjectively "in the mind" of a child. Whether it is real or imaginary, the loss is painful all the same. Having suffered in childhood, the phobic lives in an alert state, in permanent anxiety of a new separation. The person is not conscious of this menace, nor of the worry of a new abandonment. Rather, what *is* feared is a danger from outside, such as the street, the bridge, the plane, etc., and the dangers that, according to the patient, have no relationship to the infantile trauma. Lea, for example, paralyzed by a phobia of open spaces, did not know how the anxiety was provoked by the sudden "departure" of her mother. And yet, from the moment when I brought her to relive that scene of abandonment, which was a result of my own reliving it, her fear of the streets faded. Why? Because all childhood trauma, relived, verbalized, and signified in the current moment of treatment, loses its virulence. When the trauma stays forgotten, it is harmful, but the moment it reenters consciousness it becomes harmless.

The example of Lea shows how I relived in myself, and in turn induced a reliving in the patient, of the emotion of a forgotten abandonment.

Does the psychoanalyst work as much with the heart as with reason?

More so with the heart and, I would say, with the unconscious. When I listen to the patient and I concentrate on reviving the repressed emotion, I engage, quite intentionally, my personal unconscious. The unconscious of the psychoanalyst is the most precious of all tools with which he works. To act from the unconscious is to allow the subtle vibrations from the unconscious of the patient to reverberate in the unconscious of the analyst. This immersion in oneself, necessary to meet the submerged turmoil of another, has often made me think of the divers in the film by Luc Besson, *Le Grand Bleu* (*The Big Blue*). When I am listening acutely, I have the impression of free-diving into the abyss. I try to flush out from within my own depths the traumatic scenes of the patient in order to then come back to the surface to tell her, at the right moment, with the right words, what I saw. This moment is the decisive intervention of psychoanalytic treatment, one that, it must be emphasized, *does not* happen at every meeting. It is a fascinating psychical act, but it is also one that is indispensable for one to know the origin of the suffering of another and to be able to reveal it to her. I will add that the success of this internal descent depends on a detailed knowledge of the history of the patient, a complete openness, a long clinical training, and above all, a complete personal analysis.

On the subject of psychical diving, I always think of a little-known phrase of Freud's that I believe perfectly defines the way the psychoanalyst makes use of his or her unconscious. Freud wrote, "The psychoanalyst captures the unconscious of the patient with his own." Said another way, when the psychoanalyst submerges into his own depths, he uses his unconscious as a sensory organ, one that perceives the unconscious feelings of the patient. This engagement is the psychoanalyst's greatest commitment to advance his unconscious, as sort of screen, on which the patient can project his or her childhood traumatic scenes. As such, at the most intense moments of listening, when the psychoanalyst uses his unconscious instrumentally, the psychoanalyst is suspended between being master of the situation and exploring his or her own unconscious experience. It is undoubtedly difficult to understand such a split of consciousness and experience. It is something one must experience to understand: to feel perfectly lucid, and at the same time, to be submerged in one's unconscious.

How do you differentiate between psychoanalytic technique as you have just described it and that of psychotherapy?
There is a great difference between the two methods. The listening of a psychologist consists of unraveling a relational conflict while identifying the past and present events that have provoked it. It is

a work of useful clarification that allows the patient to understand the significance of his or her conflicts, and the reason behind their repetition. The listening of the psychoanalyst is very different. It is not only a matter of bringing the patient to understand the relationship between situations that end in conflict, but to incite him or her to relive—as I have just shown you—the emotional upheaval that generates the current suffering. That said, the same practitioner in the course of a cure could use both techniques, in spite of their differences. A psychoanalyst could legitimately begin treatment, as would a psychologist, and then, if the state of the patient demands it, begin to apply the psychoanalytic technique of using the analyst's own unconscious to capture that of the patient.

What are the advantages of one technique over another?
While psychotherapy is a kind of listening that is capable of provisionally removing the symptom, psychoanalysis not only obtains the same beneficial results, but it above all changes the personality of the patient by bringing about a change in his or her attitude toward his or her suffering. When an analysis is effective, it directs the patient to change the very worldview that had made him or her sick. Psychoanalysis teaches him how to go into him or herself and discover the stranger in himself in order to regard him or herself differently and to re-experience his or her illness. "The true birthplace," wrote Marguerite Yourcenar, "is that wherein, for the first time, one intelligently looks upon oneself."[2]

You said, "changes the personality" but doesn't that risk destroying the patient?
I will answer you by citing the words of a patient who recently wrote me after a session. He said to me, "In the work that you do with me, you do not destroy, you do not repair, you do not replace, you do not add, you reinforce the existent." In effect, the principle that guides me is expressed in these terms: the patient, delivered from his or her harmful conflicts, should reconcile with him or herself, find him or herself on the basis of that which he or she is. My goal is not to change the personality, but to enrich it with what he or she already has in him or herself, and if possible, to teach him or her to love him or herself differently. Take for example an artist, who states during the first session that irrespective of the reason that

brought him or her to therapy, he or she fears his or her artistic inspiration would fade during the cure. I would reassure the patient that I will not take away nor add anything to who he or she is and I would affirm that I will try to stimulate in him or her all of their creative potential.

JOËL, OR MY FEAR OF DISCOVERING
A CASE OF PSYCHOSIS

How do we define mental health? When do you say that a person is psychologically healthy?
Your question speaks to a number of debates and explorations at the heart of the community of mental health professionals, so I can only offer you a quick response.

In my view, mental health is *the state of a person capable of knowing his or her limits and who loves and accepts them.* To be psychologically healthy signifies that one lives relatively happily with oneself, in spite of the inevitable challenges, surprises, and restrictions that life imposes. Mental equilibrium can be seen as having the will to take action, while having the ability to accept the unexpected and to adapt.

What do you think of madness? Do you believe that recent neuroscientific advances can claim a decisive victory over mental illness?
We are going too quickly! Don't forget that current research in mental health is, sadly, far behind medical research in general. You know that psychiatry and psychology are relatively young sciences. Mathematical study can be traced back to ancient Greece; physics has had already five centuries of existence; chemistry appeared in the eighteenth century; biology is nearly as old; but psychiatry and psychology can be dated at the beginning of the nineteenth century. Recall that madness was not always a synonym of mental illness. It was during the Renaissance that madmen were no longer seen as people possessed by demons and had an illness that deserved treatment, and not exorcism. Medical treatments began to be tested, albeit rather primitive versions. The Renaissance was the era where healers practiced a fraud called "*pierre de tête.*" I am thinking of the famous Flemish picture where one can see the work of one of these

charlatans. After having shaved the head of a demented patient and made an incision in the skin on his skull, he then made a show of extracting a bloody stone; a stone that had certainly been stashed in his pocket before the "operation." There is also in the Prado museum a painting by Hieronymus Bosch that is a representation of a similar scene, titled *The Extraction of the Stone of Madness*.

No, we are neither omniscient nor infallible! Our current knowledge of the psyche is still incomplete. Even with the contributions of psychoanalysis and neuroscience, we continue to miss the actual causes of mental illness. We work with hypotheses perfectly formed, we have vastly refined our means of helping patients, and above all we dispense powerful medicine, but, and this is totally unknown to the public, we still do not know how schizophrenia, manic-depressive psychosis or delirium begins and develops. I can tell you without hesitation that we ignore the developmental process of mental illness and, a fortiori, the active mechanism in our medications. We prescribe psychotropic medication that is becoming increasingly capable of mitigating a delirium or of liberating the schizophrenic from an overwhelming hallucination, and nevertheless, we do not know by which neurochemical chain reaction a particular molecule makes a particular symptom disappear. Moreover, do not forget that at the moment that I speak to you there does not exist a psychotropic drug that will heal someone completely. All of our medications have a palliative effect, but never a completely curative one. The medication can suppress the symptom, but it does not suppress the cause of the symptom.

The limit of our knowledge makes us sometimes feel desperately powerless before the intensity of our patients. I saw families trapped for years in a drama because their child had suffered from schizophrenia who oscillated between getting better and getting worse, going back and forth to the hospital. These same parents, who had fought like lions to help at the beginning of the child's symptoms, I later found to be exhausted and destroyed. They revealed a desire to see their child commit suicide so that they could be at last delivered from the madness that threatened them as well.

At the same time, I would like to be clear that outside of these extreme cases, we are beginning to see a reduction in the number of relapses, shorter hospital stays, and an improved rehabilitation program that makes patients more autonomous and better integrated in society, thanks to the work of polyvalent therapies.

As a psychoanalyst, how do you approach mental illness?
Instead of a direct answer, I will tell you about one of my clinical experiences. A long time ago, I saw Joël, who was seventeen years old and accompanied by his parents. As is my habit, I asked that his mother and father stay in the waiting room while I interviewed the son first one-on-one. Joël was a talkative boy, very athletic, who adored tennis. He explained to me that he could no longer go to school because of a paralyzing anxiety. Often, when he would arrive at the entrance to the school, he thought he would faint; panicked, he would quickly lie down. A particular softness and tremendous suffering that I could see in his face brought about in me an immediate desire to help him.

By discussing this case, I would like you to understand the difficulty I face when I have a patient like Joël, for I always fear that I will find an irreparable psychic break. When I encounter such a touching and sensitive child, I am taken by a secret fear that I will find in him the monster that is insanity. From the first interview, I have an imperative need to know if his inner being is broken, or if it remained intact. For me, patients that have mental trouble are schematically divided into two large categories. There are those that suffer because an internal mechanism is broken—I am thinking of psychotics—the mechanism of rupturing is what Lacan called *"foreclosure."* There are those that suffer while nothing essential is wounded—I am thinking of neurotics—the mechanism at work is *"repression."* This is why I was profoundly concerned that I might discover in Joël the beginnings of a psychosis hiding behind his phobia of school. I live with the same unease as an oncologist, who, when examining a patient with care, looks for a tumor with the hope of never finding one. This is the same attitude I adopt: I draw upon all of my knowledge of psychoanalysis in order to discover a fault that, with all my being, I do not want to find: the psychic fracture. To discover a psychic fracture in this young man, to discover that he suffers from a burgeoning schizophrenia, would be to recognize the beginning of a drama that could last his entire life, a life of a martyr. I should tell you that with Joël, I was relieved to discover that his suffering was not one of an irreversible psychosis, but of a phobia, albeit a serious one.

If you asked me, "But how did you know that it was neurotic phobia and not a latent psychosis?" I would tell you that I knew it by posing certain questions to Joël—simple but precise. For example

I asked him: "Can you concentrate when you study?" He affirmed, "Yes, I have no problems, but occasionally I freeze up and my mind goes blank." And then I insisted, "But when this happens, or if you must make a huge effort to understand what you read, do you feel pain in your head? Do you have pain in your neck or the top of your back?" He replied, "No."

Waiting for his denial, I was reassured. If, for example, Joël had responded that he had to force himself to concentrate to the point of having a headache while showing me where he had the pain, and if he had talked to me about his suffering, that would have been for me the first suspicion of a burgeoning psychosis. Why? Because one of the first indicating signs of a schizophrenic formation is an enormous difficulty concentrating, accompanied by a hypochondriacal pain, that is to say an imaginary, hallucinated, pain, which young patients often locate around the neck and top of the back.

To eliminate my concerns, I further asked, "When you look in a mirror, do you sometimes have the impression that your body is changing, that your face is no longer yours or that your nose is deformed?" He replied, "No." So I asked further, "And your hands? Do you sometimes have the impression that they have changed?" "No," he assured me. If on the contrary, he had said, "Yes, sometimes I look at my hands and they seem strange to me," that would have indicated the beginning of depersonalization, the first step toward the diagnosis of an embryonic schizophrenia.

If Joël had responded in this way, I would have had to inform his parents of the extent to which they would have to attend to their son's needs and that I would need their cooperation to help him get better, since the participation of the parents is indispensable for the treatment of young psychotics.

This is how I approach a case of psychosis. But, as you may well imagine, in everyday practice, I would not formulate a diagnosis until there had been many meetings with the patient.

You have asked me about the role psychoanalysis plays in the treatment of mental suffering. It depends on the type of problem to be treated. Recall the distinction that I proposed between two types of suffering: One in which the psychical apparatus is out of balance but intact (neurosis), the other in which it is damaged (psychosis). Of course, psychoanalysis is a treatment that is most effective when the psychical apparatus remains intact, but when the soul is broken, the analytic cure is a necessary complement to a medical treatment, including inpatient care in an institution. That is how the combined action of individual and familial psychoanalysis, with medication and hospitalization, came about as the best therapeutic strategy for patients that have succumbed to a painful psychical fracture.

HOW DOES ONE CHOOSE A PSYCHOANALYST?

The public is often confused by the different kinds of mental health professionals. How do we distinguish between a psychologist, a psychiatrist, and a psychoanalyst?
It is true that for the average person the distinction between the three is not always easy to make. I can tell you that a psychologist is a person with a university degree in psychology. A psychologist can work in a number of sectors, such as schools, businesses, and general hospitals, as well as mental hospitals, prisons, and nurseries. He or she can also see patients in his or her office and practice various methods of therapeutic treatment, including psychoanalysis.

The psychiatrist is a medical specialist with a medical degree. A psychiatrist is a doctor who cares for psychotics, depressives, or neurotics in an inpatient or outpatient environment. Psychiatrists can prescribe medication and can also choose a "talking cure" according to the principles of psychotherapy or psychoanalysis, but need not necessarily do so. I will add that there are doctors who have pursued degrees in higher education who may have no relation to psychology, but they can later train in psychoanalysis and treat people accordingly. But whether or not one is a psychologist, a psychiatrist, or a practitioner from another subfield, they cannot practice psychoanalysis except under the following conditions: they must have completed a personal analytic treatment, have thoroughly studied the fundamental psychoanalytic texts, and discussed the application of psychoanalytic theory with a senior colleague who oversees and guarantees the quality of work with the patients. Note that a psychoanalyst is one of the rare professionals who during the first ten, or perhaps even twenty years of activity must present each week to a supervising psychoanalyst and give a detailed account of the treatment he or she carries out with his or her patients. Psychoanalysis is a therapeutic practice that can be exercised by a psychologist, a psychiatrist, or any other professional who has satisfied these conditions.

I have just said psychoanalysis is a therapeutic practice, but be aware that it is not a medical one. A psychoanalyst is certainly a clinician who is attentive to psychological and somatic symptoms when these express psychical conflicts, since he or she knows the extent to which the body notably echoes the unconscious. Nevertheless, somatic symptoms are not studied in a medical sense by a psychoanalyst. The psychoanalyst does not prescribe psychotropic medication, even though he or she knows the uses. His or her knowledge of medication, albeit incomplete, permits him or her to speak a common language with other health care professionals for example, when treating someone who needs hospitalization. I insist that psychoanalysis is not a field of medicine, but many of our patients also follow a medical treatment, which obliges us to know about the latest pharmacological research.

And yet, beyond the therapeutic activity, psychoanalysis has always been influenced by multiple cultural and social movements. For a hundred years it has not ceased to influence the domains of art, literature, philosophy, and sociology. Psychoanalysis has definitively left its mark in the field of education by helping us better understand child psychology, and it participated actively in the elimination of insane asylums by recognizing the dignity of the mentally ill.

So then what is the commonality amongst the various aspects of psychoanalysis?
I can answer without hesitation: it is the unconscious. As long as there are humans involved, so too will be the unconscious. Why is this? Well, what is it to be human? The singular trait of the human being is not speech, thought, or laughter, but that he or she is powerless at mastering the forces that act on the person from within, whether beneficial or harmful. The forces that elude us, and that exceed our will and our conscious knowledge, all fall under the heading of the unconscious.

And so, the proper work of psychoanalysis is to be concerned with the unconscious when the unconscious makes us suffer, that is to say, when the difference between who we are, and that which exceeds us, makes us unhappy.

You describe the vast influence of psychoanalysis, but what are its limits?
I will remind you that above all, Freud defined psychoanalysis as an investigative process of psychical life, a therapeutic method, and a theory that results from these practices. Of these three facets, it is above all the therapeutic method that demonstrates best the success and the limits of psychoanalysis. I have had the satisfaction, as have many of my colleagues, of treating many patients whose often serious problems definitively disappear. I have received many letters from former patients that tell me of a marriage that was previously unimaginable, the birth of a child much awaited, and many other testimonies of the efficaciousness of the psychoanalytic cure! Incontestably, psychoanalysis is an excellent way of easing suffering, but like all techniques, there are constraints for those who undergo it.

What constraints?
The constraints that frequently give rise to three main complaints, the first being: "Psychoanalysis is a *long, expensive,* and *painful* treatment." In effect, an analytic cure *can* last several years, but that depends on the relationship between the analyst and the analysand. For my part, my adult cases last two to three years. When couples consult me regarding problems they have living together, I schedule a series of successive sessions spread out over a period of about six months. If it concerns a child, I prefer to limit the number of visits as much as possible. This prevents the young patient from becoming so excessively dependent that the analytic relationship would replace the necessary familial dependence. The treatment of a child, if recommended, would last on average between six months and two years, depending on the severity of the symptoms.

The second complaint against analysis concerns the cost. On this point, I know that to undergo a treatment requires a significant financial commitment. Even though our rates are often adapted to the patient's ability to pay, there is still the difficulty of budgeting for two sessions a week. But such an expense pales in comparison to the vital importance of what brings someone into therapy: self-defeating behavior, sexual trouble, marital problems, difficult relations with a child, depression, etc. One must understand that analysis is sometimes the last resort for a desperate person, and that the possibility of a cure is crucial for the person. Also, do not forget that there is help for those without resources at open clinics and other open institutions.

The last critique is that of the painful nature of psychoanalysis. Without a doubt, the patient goes through periods of intense emotion and can leave the session quite upset. Without a doubt, analysis has moments when memories are painfully relived, and you can imagine that no one could bear the treatment if all the sessions were painful. We can also say that we share moments of happiness with the patients, and we sometimes laugh together, in the moments when it is a pleasure to reconstruct their history, take account of progress to date, or imagine the future.

If the relationship between patient and therapist is this powerful and intimate, then the choice of the psychoanalyst is crucial. What advice can you give others in finding the right person?
It is a question people often ask me. When we measure the intensity of the engagement that psychoanalysis entails, one must indeed take the greatest care in choosing a therapist. How *can* one proceed to find the right therapist?

I can begin by stating what one should *not* do, namely, to choose a therapist based on the school to which he or she belongs. In all groups there exist good and bad practitioners. I can be critical of a school of analysis, and at the same time recognize talented practitioners in that school. As I see it, the personal qualities of the therapist are infinitely more important than the school of thought to which they subscribe.

Apart from this concern, what is then the best criterion for choosing a psychoanalyst? I will tell you that the best path is simply to go and consult with a psychoanalyst who has been recommended to you. Most importantly, evaluate the effects the first encounter has on you. Perhaps it will be necessary to consult two or three therapists before making a decision, but no more than that; one should avoid seeing too many (I have known of people who saw up to eight!). This has an impact on one's ability to judge, because on the third or fourth attempt the patient is accustomed to telling his story and becomes desensitized. The patient loses the spontaneity and anxiety that is appropriate to the success of the first encounter.

The best criterion on which to make a decision as a future patient is based on the impression one has at the very first encounter with the psychoanalyst. One must feel relieved and confident, while noting that the therapist was able to articulate clearly what I was feeling in a confused manner. What follows is what determines the best therapist for someone: the secret conviction that the psycho-analyst has understood me and is ready to help me. In a word, the feeling that the therapist I just met had already helped me. Thus, leaving the preliminary session, patients tell themselves, "*I already feel better. This psychoanalyst has given me hope and has given me the strength that I need now.*" The patient does not say, "*It is him or her that I will choose,*" but rather, "*I have the desire to see him or her again because I sense that my life's path will be changed.*"

Now, in order to create an environment for this kind of good will, it is preferable that the therapist speaks in the final minutes of the initial session. I counsel all of my students to conclude the first session by communicating to the patient the deep significance of what was heard. It is indispensable, before the end of the first session, to reformulate in different words the substance of the complaint that one heard from the patient. Indeed, we should show the patient that his or her way of interpreting his or her suffering is perhaps not the most adequate, and that there is another approach. I have found these parting words on the part of the psychoanalyst the best way of welcoming the patient while establishing a productive transferential relationship.

In sum, the best criterion for finding the right psychoanalyst is to experience right away the clear desire to return to see him or her again.

But is psychoanalysis a valuable method for everyone? Who is analyzable and who is not? And why?
The topic you bring up, of "analyzability," has often stirred up the analytic community. I will tell you the substance of my position. First of all, know that psychoanalysis is not a method that can be applied to everyone; it is not the case that everyone can be analyzed. What then are the conditions of analysis, and what is the profile of a person who is open to the benefits of this treatment? In order to be analyzed one must meet certain conditions. First, the man, woman, or child must be a subject who suffers beyond what he or she can

bear. In addition, they must complain about this fact. The complaint is crucial. Second, it is someone who asks why they are tormented to such an extent. That may seem elementary, but it is decisive. In order to be analyzed, one must ask the question, "Why do I suffer? Why am I doing so poorly?" And one must attempt to find for oneself the answer to the question. The third condition is precisely that attempt to explain one's suffering.

To suffer, to ask about the cause of the suffering, and to try to understand it, are the necessary conditions for a true engagement in an analysis. But there are other conditions that are just as important. It is also necessary that the person seeking analysis believe that the psychoanalyst holds the key to understanding his or her problems. This belief is fundamental, because it is synonymous with hope, and as we know, hope is one of the forces that drive the cure until the pain is eased. From a theoretical point of view, Lacan has synthesized this confidence in the analysis and the psychoanalyst in an eloquent formula: "*Sujet-supposé-Savoir* [Subject-supposed-to-Know]." We can modify this expression with "the psychoanalyst-supposed-to-know," a psychoanalyst that we think is sufficiently competent to help us find a way out. The patient expects his or her recovery with a psychoanalyst, who is believed to be capable of achieving said recovery. To expect is already to believe that there will be a happy ending. Everything hinges on the belief that the therapist will know how to respond. You see, it is only as a result of the promise of my healing the patient—a promise that in fact the psychoanalyst has never actually made, but I imagined was made—that the treatment can then begin.

The last condition of analysis may surprise you: it is a matter of anxiety. In fact, even if that seems curious to you, it is necessary that the person seeking treatment hesitates to confide and is wary about getting involved in analysis. Yes, one should have anxiety and fear of confiding. Without that, psychoanalytic action would have no chance of being successful.

Let me explain by describing an initial consultation I had where this fear was missing. Recently I received in my office a well-known businessman. He was around forty years old, elegantly dressed, and arrived at my office in a chauffeured limousine. Immediately in the waiting room, without the least hesitation, he started talking loudly on his cell phone. Later, when he entered my office with a self-assured air, he sat down on the chair with the arrogance of someone who fears nothing. In a businesslike tone, he proceeded to speak of his interest in receiving practical advice and counsel. My first words to him were designed to establish the boundaries of our relationship, and to ask that he not use his cell phone in the waiting room:

"The next time, when you are waiting, I prefer that you sit and meditate. When you open the front door, I ask that you inhabit the space as though it is your own internal world, as if when you pass the threshold you are no longer in an office, but in a dream. It is as if you are dreaming. Imagine that it is the moment when you go to bed and turn out the lights. It is this instant, this brief moment of time between waking and sleep that I want you to relive here. As such, when you arrive next time, peacefully find a place to sit and try to collect yourself."

Of course, I formulated the remarks in a cordial and respectful tone, and he received them well because he was presumably looking for just such an act of authority. By coming to see me, he was hoping, without knowing it, that someone would speak to the child in him, apart from his social position.

You can see that the lack of anxiety, I mean, the cavalier attitude of the patient, is a stumbling block to analysis. It was for this reason that I proposed a limited series of sessions without inviting him to lay down on the couch. I waited for the time, however many visits it would take, for him to ask, *"Doctor, why haven't you asked me to lie down on the couch?"* I told him that one must be patient and the couch would be recommended depending on the evolution of the discussions. In order to be able to lie down, the patient needs a certain capacity to go into himself and become aware of the drives of his internal life. There are many people who do not know or cannot meditate on their internal life, and instead are always focused on the external. This leap into oneself is a very difficult exercise for people of action, while other patients who may be manifestly more anxious, know how to question themselves. For those who are conscious of their unhappiness, the couch remains the most effective method.

On the subject of those who go to a psychoanalyst, I would like to point out that the majority are motivated by their difficulties, not by a desire to be analyzed. It is an error to think those who seek help explicitly want an analytic cure. Above all, they are most concerned with being rid of their unhappiness and not with the methods used, whether it goes by the name psychotherapy or psychoanalysis. What they want is not to suffer anymore. After the first few visits, it falls to the psychoanalyst to adapt his or her technique to the particulars of each patient.

I would like to conclude with a lucid phrase from Lacan: "What people ask from us, we should say in the plainest terms possible, is happiness."

AIMANCE, OR THE NEED TO BE DEPENDENT

There is another criticism we make of psychoanalysis, that of creating and sustaining the dependency of the patient.
But analysis cannot even begin to take place without a relation of dependence! It is necessary that the patient has a desire to go to the appointments and be as intimate as possible; otherwise the treatment has no chance of succeeding. I know the contemporary view is that such a dependency has pejorative connotations, but in an analytic relationship the dependence of the patient is, on the contrary, positive, necessary, and I would even say, inescapable. It is impossible for a patient to voice his innermost secrets without being connected to the listener. And one is strongly attached to the person who helps one recognize the stranger in oneself. When someone helps us to go inside ourselves and discover a forgotten emotion, it is inevitable that he be loved. In sum, if a person confides regularly in another, it will lead to his being attached to the other. This is what I want you to see: the phenomenon of dependence cannot be disassociated from the content of the analytic relationship.

I would, however, like to add an important observation: any affective dependence, whether it is analytic or not, is a response to the primary need for attachment. In effect, our bodies are always hungry for another body and our souls thirsty for another soul. In youth, we all have been and have gone through an essential dependence to the nourishing mother. From our earliest years, we are driven by an imperious need to attach ourselves to somebody, to tie ourselves to a select few to whom we attribute the force of a protective authority. It is as if we are always moved by a healthy parasitic drive, by a propensity to take hold of another, and to confer on him or her a guardian power. We attach ourselves to him and apply our capacity to love, hate, or fear. Our lives are aimed at those special few, parents, professors, friends, partners, children, therapists, on whom we are dependent because they let us love them, hate them, or fear them. I call the force that incites us to depend on another, the object of our emotions: *need of dependence, attachment drive*, or, more poetically, *aimance*. In this expression *aimance*, I have collapsed the words "*aimer*" (to love) and "*tendance*" (tendency) in order to designate the force that pushes us into the arms of our partners to the extent that we are dependent. I recall the spontaneous declaration of a young female patient who exclaimed, "I sense in me an overflowing love that only wants to go toward someone who I will make my master!"

Many times it has happened to me, while listening to a patient during the first appointment, that I will be able to measure the intensity of his or her *aimance*. Beyond the words used, I hear the patient tacitly inquire of me, "Are you available for me to love, hate, or fear? May I idealize you? Will you accept being honored one day and mistreated the next? Are you ready to enter my fantasies and play a role?" Without question, those who we solicit are drawn by an insatiable need to find a sentimental benefactor and attach themselves.

But I have also told you that affective dependence was necessary for the success of treatment, as it renders the patient more receptive to the interventions of the psychoanalyst. If the patient is not dependent, if the therapist is not idealized as an infallible elder, the patient will not feel sufficiently confident to free his or her unconscious.

That being the case, the psychoanalytic practitioner should master the spontaneous phenomenon of dependence, both in its intensity and duration. If the dependence becomes excessive or if the treatment goes on indefinitely, I would deduce that the therapist did not know how to direct the cure, that is to say, to maintain the right distance with his or her patient in order to avoid falling into a relationship that is as passionate as it is interminable. Certainly, such setbacks can be overcome; fortunately, they are not that frequent. Beyond these impasses, the fact remains that the dependence of the patient, properly directed by the psychoanalyst, is compulsory to all healing.

Is this attachment to the psychoanalyst the transference?

Absolutely. Transference designates all of the hostile and tender affection that bind a patient to his or her therapist. Throughout the sessions, the patient could love the psychoanalyst, feel protected by him, sometimes reject him, occasionally have sexual desire for him, include him in his fantasies or dreams, and at other times may even make him or herself distraught, fearful that the therapist will get angry or abandon him. All these feelings express the need for dependence and they originate in the presence of an intimate and steady conversation.

I often imagine that the psychoanalyst is an *attractor of feelings*, a kind of "coat rack" inviting the patient to satisfy his or her need for dependence, on which to hang his or her "emotional clothes." Other times, it appeared to me that the psychoanalyst is a punching bag on which the patient exercised repeated blows of love and hate. Well, transference is this: to be attached to a psychoanalyst who offers him or herself as the target of love and its avatars.

And the professional puts up with it?
That is his or her job! Insofar as he or she is properly installed and comfortable as a therapist, he or she is able to take the punches without being shaken. For a therapist to be properly situated in one's work, he or she must always remember that it is not that one is loved or hated for who one *is*, but for what one *represents*. It is not for our beauty or our mind that the patient loves us, nor is it for our mean-spiritedness that the patient hates us. Without a doubt, we are sensitive to the manifestations of sympathy and antipathy, but we know that they are inspired by the role that we assume, and not for who we are as a person.

Nevertheless, I recognize that everything is not revealed by transference. The human qualities of the psychoanalyst count as well. According to their personality, certain colleagues induce a paternal or maternal transference more easily. But no one is more inclined by his or her personal history to treat one type of patient or a certain type of suffering.

But why this word, "transference"?
The way we speak today, and here I think of the title of a film, *Fatal Transference* [*Mortel Transfert*], this word signifies, as I have just proposed, *a profound attachment to an idealized therapist*. I will briefly mention that this film is about a patient that is assassinated and pays with her life for her transferential love!

But to return to your question, the term *transference* has another, more technical, sense. Freud introduced it in order to indicate the love-hate of a patient for her therapist that results from a *displacement* of feeling, from the past to the present. The sentiments stay the same, but they transfer from a figure in childhood onto the therapist. For example, a given patient will think that she loves her psychoanalyst, but she ignores that in reality she loves a personality from a long time ago her psychoanalyst represents. You see the patient conflates the time period: she takes the present for the past; and she mistakes the person: she takes the psychoanalyst to be her father, her brother, or another figure from her past. "Transference" would then imply *illusion*, the illusion to think that one loves one's psychoanalyst and that it is a new moment when in reality it is the apparition of a forgotten earlier moment.

Transference is not only the expression of a need of dependence; it is also the resurgence of former feelings. The person led by *aimance* has the compelling need to attach him or herself to someone and to reproduce a complex relationship with him or her made up of love, hate, desire, and fear. Therefore, the transference means: to project an old love onto a person on whom we would like to depend. As such, transference is born of a need for dependence compounded by a return to the past.

That said, do not think that transference is manifest exclusively in a psychoanalytic relationship; it is a phenomenon inherent in all affective relations.

Are you saying that each time we love or hate we are engaging in transference?
Exactly! All of our feelings devoted to our loved ones for example, result from an instinctive transference of our childhood and adolescent turmoil. From this, a question arises: What difference is there between transference with our loved ones and transference specifically with a psychoanalyst? In order to respond, I will insist on the spontaneous characteristic of the transferential phenomenon: in the majority of our affective relations—psychoanalytic or not—we transfer without knowing it. Accordingly, when a woman is in love with a man, she does not realize that she loves him in the same way, good or bad, that she loved her own mother. Similarly, when a patient feels in sync with his psychoanalyst it is also completely unconscious that he is attached to him. But the difference between ordinary transference and analytic transference consists in this: we live our ordinary transferences in complete innocence of its existence, while analytic transference is made explicit by the practitioner. So it is the work

of the psychoanalyst that reveals the transference, by showing the patient that his affective reactions during their sessions are replications of old, childhood attitudes.

To conclude, everything comes from the past, and as we say, "plays itself out" before six years of age?
That is not the right way of putting it because that implies that, after early childhood, life is but a mechanistic repetition of what we have been. To what end would an analysis serve if everything were so regulated in advance? No, the major events of early childhood do not make the man, they only stake out a path for him to take. Without a doubt, the first years are the most decisive, but many things that take place in adolescence through adulthood can change the course of one's life.

When I told you that the work of a psychoanalyst is to reveal to the patient the undetected power of the past, do not think that it is all about history. The psychoanalyst is not a historian. It is the immediacy of the present that interests him or her, and for this reason he or she investigates the past in order to better understand the present. The psychoanalyst uses the past to assist in reviving an essential memory. Recall the case of Lea. Her symptoms were reduced the day when she had intensely relived an abandonment that, until then, had been unapproachable. This is our goal: to bring out, here and now, the unconscious of another, to reanimate a traumatic scene from the past and steer the patient to relive it fully. The rediscovered event will likely be more explosive than the original one.

If this goal is attained, the analysis will end?
In general, yes. As the patient revives old conflicts, the cure in effect winds its way to a conclusion. In addition, it is during this final period that the patient detaches him or herself from the psychoanalyst and realizes that it is not the psychoanalyst as a person that he loves, but the role that he assigned to him.

We can sum up the action of the psychoanalyst in two stages. In the first, generally longer, stage the therapist assumes the role of the attracter of sentiments, incites transference, and creates an environment for the revival of dormant feelings in the patient. Then, in a second stage, near the end of treatment, once the revival is complete, the analyst unveils the origin of the transference, and brings the patient to separate him or herself from him or her. When I told you that the practitioner masters the dependence, I was thinking of just this aptitude. To awaken transference and then have the ability to dissolve it, or if you prefer, to maintain the dependence and then to take away support for the dependence.

Do you have an example?
I am thinking of a female patient, who was far into treatment, and for whom a major problem was a painful conflict she had with men, and in particular her father. One day when she was furious with me, as had at times been the case, I recall having told her: "You are angry, exactly as you were, as an adolescent, against your father. But I am not your father. You should right now find him in yourself, confront the image you have of him and the image of yourself when you were young and in his presence. Bring it back to life and relive with him your attachment, your rancor, and your guilt. If you do this you will reconcile with him and be assuaged."

Immediately upon my intervention, the patient began to cry and was in touch with her hate and feelings of culpability. During the following session, she had a change of attitude toward me, and it appeared that she had also modified her comportment with men in general. From this session forward, we had entered into the final phase of her analysis, which was characterized by an internal detachment that released her from me and by a happy encounter with someone who would become her companion.

Why had my intervention with her been so efficacious? When unveiling the transference, by reminding her that I was not her father, I brought the patient to *re-center* her hate on the proper target—the father figure—to *feel again* the emotion fully and profoundly, and to finally *release* her from it. This is how her anger gave way to a serene sadness.

LOVE AND SEXUAL PLEASURE

THE SOLITUDE OF THE HOMOSEXUAL MALE AND THE "BITTER DELIGHT" OF THE HOMOSEXUAL FEMALE

You see a variety of people with quite different reasons for seeing you. What in your view is the principle malaise of our time? The motives for having a consultation are not as diverse as you would think. In the end, they are limited to the principle chapters of our lives: sexual difficulties, family conflicts, and work-related problems. If we look at the symptoms for which we are consulted, we find primarily the fears in people who suffer from phobias, the discouragement of depressives, the passionate and tormented affairs of hysterics, and the tortured thoughts of obsessives.

But when you ask of me to identify the main social malaise of the beginning of this century, I respond that without contest it is the preoccupying question of masculine identity. It is readily apparent that the major problem, which risks becoming even more severe, is the progressive loss of the defining features of masculinity. This is one of the most common problems that I encounter daily: many men seek help for sexual impotence, premature ejaculation, and more generally, for difficulties in finding their place in the couple, their role as a father of a family, or as the boss in a business.

Beginning with the decline of paternal authority that began in the 1970s, and continuing today with improvements in biotechnology that permits procreation without a male presence, along with the simultaneous disappearance of the automatic transmission of the name of the father to the children, men have become painfully destabilized with respect to their virility. They no longer feel a part of the masculine community and do not find social role models anymore with which they can identify. Traditionally, in a patriarchal society, men represented the values of authority and combativeness, while women were the heart of the family and took on the role of mother and spouse offering support and company. Upon acquiring a

25

legitimate professional and financial autonomy, women have irreversibly upset this schema and we had to and shall continue to rethink the entire social paradigm. At the moment I am speaking with you, there are many of us who note these changes, but we take no heed of the consequences. What will humankind be like in the future? Will the two sexes continue to unify their behavior with males emasculating themselves and females de-feminizing themselves over time? What forms will the relationship between males and females assume in the year 2090 for example? It is a mystery! It would be vexingly difficult to divine the types of relationships males and females will create in the future in order to love one another and to live together.

Beyond these profound revisions of masculine identity, however, what is certain today is the appearance of a new view of sexuality. My clinical experience confirms it. For example, when I began my work as a psychoanalyst, I saw homosexuals who asked for help in order to stop being homosexual. I have not forgotten that my very first patient suffered from being a lesbian. At that time—I was very young—I already knew that it was inconceivable to change a homosexual into a heterosexual, since it is impossible to change a declared sexual identity. Today, homosexuals no longer come for therapy in order "to be cured of their sexual inclinations," but for other motives entirely.

We know how much the gay community has gained recognition and occupies a significant place in the social landscape, as occurred during the AIDS prevention campaigns. In a short period of twenty years of striving for recognition, the homosexual movement has gained rights that would have been unimaginable before 1980. While it is true that homophobia continues to exist, it is incomparably less virulent than just a few years ago. Without a doubt the social representation of homosexuality has radically changed.

Is homosexuality still considered an illness?
No, homosexuality is neither a perversion nor an illness, but a proper modality of love, a particular manner of loving and of feeling loved. As I already mentioned, homosexuals come for therapy because they suffer, and they suffer from a serious problem, that of solitude. It has been some time since I saw in my office "Roger," a young man, a cultivated high-level bureaucrat in an important administration. He confided in me, "Doctor, I am homosexual. My parents do not know,

only my older sister knows my secret. I feel unhappy because I am desperately lonely. I have not been successful at living with someone." This is the contemporary homosexual tragedy: an emotional solitude. Even though he is socially integrated, he remains irreparably alone. His problem is not one of accepting his homosexual identity, but rather it is that of finding the love that we all need. We know that if a homosexual wants to, he can at any moment satisfy a purely physical desire. All he has to do is go to known meeting places—saunas, bars, particular parks or cinemas—in order to find a quick encounter with a temporary partner and obtain a furtive masturbatory orgasm. But affection, tenderness, tying his life to that of a companion who loves him, the simple act of brushing one's teeth in the same bathroom, running errands, or traveling together, in sum, he is missing out on the pleasures of everyday daily life and that makes him suffer as if from an open wound. This painful contrast between sexual hyperactivity and the instability of romantic feelings explains without a doubt the precariousness of young gay couples. Only older men can settle down together, nourished by mutual interest and shared projects.

How does psychoanalysis explain homosexuality in general?

There is no such thing as homosexuality in general! Notice, I only spoke to you of male homosexuality; lesbianism is quite different. To stick to the masculine question, I will begin by telling you that all men without exception have homosexual tendencies and that sexual games between boys, common at puberty, are experimental explorations that are perfectly typical. It is only when the tendencies are fixed in terms of a definitive sexual choice that we can begin to speak of homosexuality. In general, this fixation takes place around eighteen to twenty years of age.

I will take advantage of the moment to remind you that essentially we are all bisexual. Bisexuality is an innate human disposition that is both physical and psychical. However, we should be careful not to confuse this constitutive bisexuality with bisexual practice. It is one thing to know that each one of us harbors a masculine and a feminine part; it is another thing to make love indiscriminately with one or the other sex. Based on my clinical experience, bisexual activity is not a reflection of a natural bisexuality, but is instead an expression of homosexuality. I will go so far as to affirm that a man who has sexual encounters with men or with women indiscriminately remains underneath it all a homosexual. I mean to say that, his most entrenched impulses are not truly satisfied except in carnal contact with a male body.

On this subject, I recall "Jacques," who, after his youth as an impassioned homosexual, married a woman he loved and became a devoted father. However, against all probability, and in spite of fifteen years of untroubled heterosexuality, he left his family because he driven by an irrepressible desire to live with a man. After all, homosexual desire triumphed over eclectic bisexuality.

I have said that homosexuality is neither a vice nor a perversion and we cannot consider it as a disease. For us, the homosexual is above all a fundamentally narcissistic being, that is to say passionately attached to his body, to his image and his male organ, his own as well as his partner's. But be careful; this egocentrism is in no way a serene and complacent love of self. On the contrary, the narcissism of the homosexual makes him suffer a great deal. It is an exacerbated, cruel narcissism that makes him fragile and extremely emotional: he is sometimes so sure of himself that he is obstinate and aggressive; other times, he devalues himself to such an extent that he descends into isolation and grief.

That being the case, how do we explain masculine homosexuality? Psychoanalysis considers that homosexuality was provoked by an interruption of the sexual evolution of the boy due to an excess of maternal tenderness that overwhelmed the child. This excessive tenderness of the mother for the son—often looking to compensate for the absence of the husband—fixates the young child on the overflowing pleasure to which he cannot help but yield. Without a doubt, it is the suffocating tenderness of the mother of the future homosexual, which is the case in point. Later, the boy becomes a young man that is intensely marked by the pleasure of childhood and he will be pressed to look for the same voluptuousness and the same happiness. This search for sensuality becomes for him so omnipresent that it shapes his sense of his body and imposes on it a way of loving.

What is most notable is the refinement of the homosexual; his taste and his affective choices are dictated by an imaginary scene that constantly operates within him although he is unaware of it. It is not a scene with a definite form, rather it is a fluid, unconscious image that includes two main characters: him as a child and his mother enveloping him in a sensual embrace. I repeat that this incestuous fantasy, even though it is unconscious, determines the sexual orientation of the young man. I understand your surprise: a scene imprinted in childhood has remained buried, and is replayed by the subject unconsciously in the theater of his love life!

But what about this scene do you consider to be a homosexual fantasy?
First, you must understand that in this fiction, the mother plays the role of a seductive woman and the boy the role of a seduced child. And yet, it happens that, unbeknownst to him, the homosexual projects this fantasy into the reality of his actual relationships. He plays, and makes his partner play, either role of mother and son. If he takes the role of the seductive mother, then his partner will play the role of the seduced child and vice versa. The playing out of the incestuous seduction fantasy explains why certain homosexuals look for partners who resemble the child that they were. Thus, by loving his partner, the homosexual loves himself the way his mother loved him.

I should still clarify that the seductress of the fantasy is neither the real mother of the homosexual, nor her likeness, but the character that he invented based on the real person who is his mother. The image consists of an ambiguous and dominating figure, somewhat maternal and somewhat masculine, that psychoanalysts call the "phallic mother." It is this phallic representation of the seductive mother that the homosexual identifies with or identifies his partner with.

In closing, I will describe a further explanation regarding the origin of homosexuality. It is a perspective focused not on the mother, but on the brother, that is to say on "*sameness.*" I will sum it up in a word of advice for therapists: "When treating a male homosexual patient, think of his brother. And if he does not have one, think of his virtual brother." I think in effect that the incidence of fraternity on the genesis of homosexuality is decisive and that the love for a partner is often the repetition of the passionate love for a brother. I should add: an envied and hated brother. This may seem complicated, but in the history of the homosexual, I frequently notice the following sequence: first, hostility for a rival brother, then a love for the same brother, then a love for a man. This is why I should say that masculine homosexuality results from the transformation from an old fraternal hatred to a love for someone who is similar. The homosexual prefers to love "the same" rather than be anguished by "difference," by the strange and obscure feminine body.

What, then, is the fantasm of the lesbian?

Above all, we must distinguish between two kinds of lesbians: those that declare it very early, between the ages of twelve or thirteen years, who will never change and will never know heterosexuality; and those who on the contrary were originally heterosexuals, and then became lesbians during a period of their lives, and who then sometimes rediscover their heterosexuality.

The first are women with a masculine appearance, who have never had heterosexual relations, and who have a profound aversion for those who have a penis. They abhor men, such as they imagine them: obscene, brutal, arrogant, cowardly, and boastful. But one must understand that their rejection of man is not a rejection of virility. On the contrary, they idealize virility and appropriate it. They feel as if they are an embodied example of pure virility, perfectly exempt of all deficiencies of the male gender, and superior to ordinary men. This ideal being with which they identify is in truth a hybrid figure, composed of one part male and one part maternal. It is an unusual combination of masculine mother, protector, and instructor.

One can consider that these women with a "masculine" lesbianism adjust their love lives to an unconscious scene where they play the role of the masculine mother and make their partners play the complementary role of a doleful little girl who is firmly and tenderly loved.

The other mode of lesbianism that we can qualify as "feminine," corresponds to those that let themselves be introduced to the pleasure of love without a penis. These are women who lived a heterosexual life, often married, sometimes with children, who disappointed by a man, fall passionately in love with a partner who is both strong and tender, embodying all virtues both masculine and feminine. If this passion is extinguished, it frequently the case that "feminine" lesbians return and recommit to being with a man.

We can distinguish between two types of lesbians: those of the "masculine" type that are identified with an asexual and maternal man; and those of the "feminine" type that identify with a lovesick little girl. In spite of their reciprocity, these two categories of women do not always form a couple. Many lesbian relationships are founded on motivations that are complex and subtle.

That being the case, what strikes me most is that in the amorous ties between women, there is a knot of infinite tenderness, nostalgia, and a mutual frailty. Whereas two men come together around an erect member, two women love each other around a lack and they taste, as was so beautifully written by Colette, *"the bitter delight of feeling the same, insignificant, and forgotten."*[1]

JEALOUSY: THE IMPOTENT MAN, THE ABANDONED WOMAN

If you would, could you revisit the heterosexual man and his loss of identity?
While the male homosexual assumes his identity and fights for it, the heterosexual is at a loss for an identity, and searches for a new image of masculinity. I should say, "searches for himself," because there is no longer a masculine ideal with which he can identify. Profoundly disoriented in his search for his identity, contemporary men are haunted by an agonizing question. A question that I will formulate, inspired by Freud, when he professed his ignorance of the eternal feminine: One day when he was speaking with Marie Bonaparte, the great pioneer of French psychoanalysis, he confided, "The great question that has never been answered and which I have not yet been able to answer, despite my thirty years of research into the feminine soul, is 'What does a woman want?'"[2] Today, a century later, the question of feminine desire remains unanswered and we are now facing a another question which is equally enigmatic regarding the eternal masculine, which I will paraphrase as, *"What can a man do"*—and not— "What does man want?"

The problem for a woman is that of wanting [*vouloir*] and the problem for a man is that of being able [*pouvoir*]. Lets consider this carefully. In our formulation, the word "to be able" [*pouvoir*] is not a synonym of political or social power; it expresses rather the personal conviction that a man who is capable of accomplishing an action experiences. The question, *"What can a man do?"* condenses all of the permutations of masculine doubt to the test, "Am I up to the task? Will I succeed? Am I sufficiently prepared?" I define masculine anxiety as the fear of not being able to satisfy the expectations of an other. What other? Above all a woman, or a man, invested with authority.

The man who comes for a consultation these days is a worried and destabilized person. He is an impotent, premature ejaculator, in an awkward position with his companion who was recently promoted and suddenly better paid than he, or he no longer knows how to be a parent to his children or preserve his pride with his friends; man today is at a loss as to what he has to offer and he thinks that he is unworthy of love. He wants to be loved not for that which he is but for that which he can be, give, or do. In fact, for a man, the real power resides not in the possession of material things or his place in a hierarchy, but in his ability to draw from himself more than he effectively has in him. That is power: to be capable of challenging oneself, to propel oneself toward the future.

And women?

Women are not caught in the same problem as men. From a psychoanalytic point of view, feminine sexual identity is constructed all during life and without many identity crises. A woman does not cease becoming a woman, while man consolidates his masculine identity between six and fifteen years of age even if, as I have just said, his virility can be painfully called into question. In women, the sense of femininity is never acquired; it is constantly being developed, even after the experience of motherhood. It is as if the particularity of feminine identity was to be enriched over time, not only in contact with other women, but also, and above all with men. Assuredly, that which makes a woman feel like a woman is the hand of her partner that caresses and supports her, the voice that recognizes, or the look that impassions. The intervention of the man in the formation of the feminine character is evidently decisive.

But, although it is true that the woman benefits from a sexual identity that is relatively stable, she fears, on the other hand, that her partner will abandon her. If the vulnerable point of man is power, then that of the woman is love. The malaise of a woman is the fear of being betrayed by the one she loves. This is a fear that often condemns her to solitude, because by this fear, she refuses to engage in an amorous relationship. Many of patients consult me for this reason. I recall the case of a well-known flautist, a very beautiful woman with indisputable charm, but who, at thirty-seven years of age, despaired at living alone. In spite of many attempts, she never succeeded at forming a relationship, and was panicked by the idea of tying herself to a man who would leave her in the end. This is quintessential feminine anxiety: the fear of abandonment, which, if it does lead to solitude, will foment into jealousy.

Would women be therefore more jealous than men?
Not "more jealous," but rather, they are jealous in a different way. Women do not hesitate to frequently and overtly exhibit their fear of being cheated on, as if this jealously was a natural expression of femininity. Certainly, men are just as jealous, but their suspicion manifests itself in crises and in well-defined circumstances.

Feminine and masculine jealousies are distinguished also by their content. The first is the anguish of experiencing loss; the other the greed of possessing. While the woman is jealous because of the fear of being abandoned, man is jealous from the desire to dominate; she fears solitude and he the humiliation of being stripped of his possession. As such, each form of jealousy is dominated by one of the two essential characteristics: desire and fear. For what is jealousy if not a painful feeling that condenses the fear of being betrayed and the desire to possess? In sum, jealousy is fear compounded by a feverish egoism.

Do not forget that jealousy, given its potential to be ravaging, is a perfectly normal feeling, for there is not love without jealousy. Love is naturally possessive and what is proper to the lover is the demand for exclusivity. Thus, jealousy is an exacerbation of a lover's possessiveness, the zealous guardian of the fidelity of the loved one.

When does normal jealousy turn into pathological jealousy?
At the moment when it permeates the life of the couple and is manifested in violent acts that direct the one who is jealous to destroy that which is most dear, the love of his partner. It is as if the subject traps the loved one in a cruel dilemma: "Either you belong to me, or I will destroy you." In this extreme form, the jealous state is like a state of delirium where the sick person is enclosed in his or her unreality.

At this stage, jealousy is a haunting obsession and the jealous person is sick from doubt. His torture comes from not knowing if he has or has not actually been betrayed, and he constantly asks himself:

"Is she unfaithful or is it I who am delirious?" This reminds of the words of a patient in the throes of jealousy: "I preferred to know once and for all that he had cheated on me than to put up with the hellish uncertainty that gnaws at me. At its core, my problem is not that of having been betrayed but of not knowing the truth."

Whatever it may be, jealousy, normal or pathological, is a complex reaction that combines different feelings. If the jealous person in crisis could analyze herself, she would tell us, "I suffer in four ways: because I fear losing the person I love; because I feel humiliated at the idea of being betrayed; because I hate myself for not having kept his love; and finally, because I hate the thought that my loved one, excited and happy, seduced my rival. Fear, humiliation, guilt, and hate, are the cruel elements that undermine me. But beyond even that, I feel devoured by doubt and the shame of being jealous."

Can jealousy be treated?
It all depends on its intensity. Most often, ordinary jealousy is easily soothed if one brings the person to awareness of the childhood roots of his anxiety and doubts. In order to keep his partner, the best attitude is to continue to seduce her as if it was their first date. It is a matter of replacing jealousy with seduction. To make this happen, I would advise all jealous people to recall their first meetings with their partner and the feeling of trust that brought it about. On the other hand, if the jealousy proves to be chronic, violent, and expresses paranoia, the cure becomes uncertain.

A last clarification on the matter, do you make a distinction between jealousy, envy, and rivalry?
I will respond to you in the following way: Jealousy is the fear of losing what one possesses; envy is the desire for what another possesses; and rivalry is when I fight with an adversary to gain possession of that which I do not yet have.

LOVE IN THE COUPLE

In our time, more and more couples come together only to then fall apart. Is this specific to our culture, or is it part of the nature of love itself to be ephemeral? In other words, can love last?

But of course! Thank you for giving me the occasion to say this, and even to proclaim it, for the young do not seem to know it: love *can* be lasting! Not too long ago marriages were entered into for reasons having nothing to do with feelings. They were unions of pure convenience in which the spouses learned nevertheless to live together and love one another, sometimes for their entire lives. Today, when we can freely choose, and often with passion, we leave one another over the smallest dispute. With the same suddenness of falling in love, there can be equally as immediate a violent impulse to separate. It is as if the partners in the couple no longer take the time to build and reinforce their union. Life together is like a living organism that one must constantly nourish, like a plant that needs light, care, and patience. Sometimes, it withers prematurely and other times it grows vigorously. It all depends on the way in which the protagonists nurture their love life. In order to better nurture it, one must understand the logic of love. I am convinced that the success or failure of a couple rests upon a number of factors that are largely unconscious, but also on the conscious understanding the couple has of the marital relationship.

You asked me if it was possible for love to endure, and I assured you that it is possible. Now I would like to tell you about the conditions in which love can withstand the tests of time. Clearly, I do not claim to know the truth about love—no one would risk such an undertaking, even Socrates in the *Symposium*—I will simply share with you what I learned over the years of seeing couples in my practice.

My first statement is that all feelings of love evolve and mature over the years. It is obvious that we do not love one another in the same way when we are twenty as when we are sixty. Moreover, love is very different at the beginning, middle, and end of the relationship. The beginning is dominated by the happiness of being together and the desire to realize common projects, then, after the inevitable disillusionments, the readjustments take place, and one rediscovers the loved one in a new light. This is how one modifies one's way of loving. It goes without saying that in the course of a life, each person changes physically and mentally through challenges that are both regenerative and transformative. And yet, the art of having a solid relationship is to accompany the other throughout the unforeseen changes, like a dancer preserves the rhythm by adjusting his cadence to the steps of his partner. What is important is to freely evolve one's self while preserving the stability of the relationship.

Nevertheless, there are couples that weather some rather dramatic storms.

It is true. There are no couples without crises, since crises are a part of the difficult equilibrium of living together. The problem is not to avoid crises—they are inevitable—but to learn how to surmount them, find satisfaction, and look toward calmer times. Nevertheless, beyond the ability for couples to weather the storms, the survival of their union depends on other capacities. First, there is *sexual harmony*; if she is not happy the relationship is weakened and often fails. I am not saying that a couple weakened by a sexual problem will necessarily break up. I would only like to insist on the importance of sexual pleasure for the psychic well-being of the couple, in particular for the woman. I say, "for the woman," because a partner who is sexually unsatisfied is above all a woman emotionally unsatisfied who feels neglected. Why? Because in general the woman associates sex and tenderness so that for her sex is an act of love. Therefore, it is important for the partners to have sex regularly even if they are not always consumed with passionate ardor. Long periods of sexual silence are certainly harmful to the health of the couple. This is why the secret of a blossoming sexuality resides in the harmonious combination between the regularity of sexual encounters and the role of games and fantasy to rekindle desire.

But if people are not interested in making love, they should not really go so far as making themselves do it, should they!?

Yes, they should! In certain cases, an extinguished sexual desire can be rekindled as a result of regular encounters when the couple agrees to meet for that purpose. I am thinking of a couple that came to me for counsel because their sexuality was fading after seven years of marriage, while they actively wanted to have a child together. I am not going to discuss my psychoanalytic approach to this couple; I will limit myself to mentioning the solution they found at the end of one visit that allowed them to get together again. They decided in my presence to reserve Friday night for their date. This pact, which they respected regardless of its artificial nature, renewed their desire and sexual harmony.

But beyond this example, let's take up again the different elements that help protect the love in the couple. I spoke just now about "sexual harmony," but the word *harmony* is not completely sufficient. It is in fact a matter of sexual subjection, or if you prefer, of a *sexual dependence* of one on the other. Thus, in order to establish a durable relationship, it is also necessary for each partner to be sexually subjugated by the other. On this issue, I recall a phrase by Krafft-Ebing that highlights the influence of sex on the permanence of love: in order for a relationship to last, it is absolutely necessary that there be a certain degree of "sexual bondage."[3] This claim was completely confirmed by Freud: "Some measure of sexual bondage [of a woman to a man and likewise reciprocally] is, indeed, indispensable to the maintenance of a civilized marriage and to holding at bay the polygamous tendencies which threaten it . . ."[4]

A second factor in the stability of a relationship is *reciprocal admiration*: for each, the other should be the best! No matter in which arena, but my companion should be, to my eyes, the most intuitive of women, a dazzling tango dancer, or, the most formidable business woman; and, for her, I should represent the most generous of men, the best father, or a prizewinning chef of a duck *à l'orange*! The reason for admiration does not matter! What is essential is to be proud of one's partner, even for the most modest of virtues.

But the other sparks that fuel love are the daily *rituals* of the couple, the customary gestures, which are always the same whatever the mood: the good-morning kiss, the Thursday movie night, or the Saturday morning market. Whether we are angry or not, sad or cheery, we stay faithful to the invisible structure of living together. Thus, the positive force of everyday habits can carry us through the dips in mood and the inconstancy of feeling. A regrettable conflict will be quickly forgotten if we are both busy with our daily tasks.

To conclude—the last lesson of my clinical experience—I will highlight the beneficial influence that *alternating roles* has on the longevity of the couple. I am thinking, for example, of those moments when men behave like a little boy with their partner, without feeling inferior; reciprocally, the woman can act like a little girl without feeling embarrassed. These are the regressive states, generally transitory, that are absolutely indispensable for the harmony of the relationship.

I will add one more thing: a lasting union relies on the respect that each has for the privacy of the other.

Nevertheless, as you suspect, none of my comments are intended to dissipate the inexplicable magic of love. Love remains eternally unfathomable. I am certain of only one thing: the loved one is the one who gives me the most exhilarating sensation of being alive and in whom I inspire the same elation. The loved one is the person who brings out my quintessential being and who makes me happy.

I have just said the loved one make me happy, and yet I will add that is it also the one who, by her very otherness, limits me, hinders my desires, and makes me suffer. In a stable couple, that is to say in a couple with a history, the partner is the one who makes me feel more alive, but is also the most severe censor. Decidedly, the loved one has two faces, one that makes me soar and one that brings me down at the same time.

To listen to you, one would think that living together as a couple is hell!

No need to exaggerate! Let us say rather that suffering is inherent to the nature of a romantic relationship, and it is at its very core. At the heart of love lies suffering! Beyond the conflicts of the crises that all couples must endure, and the pain of the ruptures, other torments are intrinsic to love, including everyday daily torments experienced by those who love each other with passion. Whether it is jealousy, culpability, remorse, renunciation, anxiety provoked by absence or the failures of another, or simply the frustrations due to one's inability to satisfy; all of these troubles show that the best loved ones can also be the cruelest tormentors.

Are all lovers masochists then?

Absolutely not. It might surprise you, but proper mental functioning depends on a certain degree of frustration. To be frustrated is a condition of our normality. Hence the role of the partner: by gratifying and disappointing us, our partner becomes the thermostat of our moods.

Undoubtedly, this idea can be disconcerting, because we are accustomed to attributing to our partners the singular virtue of satisfying our desires and giving us pleasure. We live under an illusion, partly true, that our partners give us more than they refuse us. In fact, the other stabilizes us more by their refusal than by what they give us. The other frustrates us because, while exciting our desire, *he or she cannot* and—even if he or she could—*would not want to* satisfy us completely. Being a human, he or she cannot, and being in love,... he or she does not want to. One *cannot* because it is impossible for a human being to fulfill completely the desire of another, and one *does not want to* because as a lover, one fears getting too attached and becoming a slave. I often say love is a universal neurosis in the sense that all lovers always fear loving too much and becoming dependent. Our companion is the person who certainly knows how to excite and gratify us, but also to restrict and thereby stabilize us. This is why the loved one is not only the one who makes us happy, but also the one who frustrates as well, and in doing so, stabilizes us.

EVERY WOMAN IS A VIRGIN

What can be said about virginity today?
It is true that over the years I rarely encountered patients that came to me for a problem related to virginity or the loss thereof. Nevertheless, I can tell you that a large number of female patients, when speaking authentically of their sexuality, declare that intimately they feel like virgins. In the anatomic sense, they know perfectly well they are no longer virgins, as the hymen has disappeared. But they feel, in the depths of their being, the existence of a place inviolate and inviolable. I have just said that the hymen disappeared but physiologically that is not precisely true, in fact the hymen never disappears.

The hymen never disappears! How is that?
Men and women believe that after the loss of virginity the hymen magically vanishes. But in reality, it never goes away. Gynecologists tell us that the hymen is a fine and supple membrane that obstructs the vaginal orifice. We find this uniquely in the human species and we do not know its precise physiological function. It is usually perforated permitting the flow of the menstrual cycle. But, once torn, it gradually retracts, forming little folds on the perimeter of the entrance to the vagina. These virginal vestiges bear the charming name of "hymen lace." According to specialists, a woman, after sexual relations and childbirth, still has these traces of the virginal membrane.

Having said that, the virginity of which I am speaking is not anatomical but obviously fantasmatic instead. Many women have the personal belief that the man has never completely penetrated their bodies, nor reached the profound depths of their being. This is what I call: *the fantasm of virginity.*

Are you referring to their symbolic body?
No, I speak of the body that women live in and fantasize about. They experience it at the level of sensation and fantasize about it

with imaginary constructions. I insist that when a woman in analysis describes without reticence the feeling that she remains whole even during penetration, she confides that there is, in her deepest being, a place that is intact, intangible, and untouched.

Is it the case that even a woman who is sexually satisfied could have this impression?
Absolutely. Such a woman can know the pleasure of an orgasm, feel it fully with someone she loves, and at the same time be inhabited by the feeling, however confused, that she retains an original purity that nothing can tarnish.

How do you explain it?
I do not know how. Like Freud, I confess that a number of aspects of feminine sexuality strongly resist comprehension. Nonetheless, I propose a psychoanalytic hypothesis that remains to be verified. I think that the feeling of an irreducible virginity cannot be found except in a being— a woman—whose bodily ability is to receive another body that, inversely, has the ability to penetrate. Listening to patients taught me that only those women who experienced the sensation of receiving the penis of the man she loves can experience their sex as an envelope, a bottomless container that opens upon an ever-secret garden. In other words, the fantasy of an infinite virginity only appears in a woman in love who has experienced the ecstasy of penetration. I insist that these considerations are but hypotheses that each woman can confirm or not.

The message that the woman gives the man is therefore: "There is something in me that I do not give."
Or rather: "I will not give you all." Or better: "I offer myself, but I do not give myself entirely. Insofar as I safeguard the source of my power I feel like and am proud to be a woman." In effect, *she offers herself but does not give herself completely*, for fear of losing her most intimate sense of self.

And how does she experience this fantasm?
It is very difficult to respond because patients have an ambivalent attitude. On the one hand, they prefer to not speak of it, and on the other, they claim their imaginary virginity as the symbol of their

femininity. I will equally say for certain women the knot of feminine identity is constructed around this place that is silent and empty. It is as if to be a woman consisted in preserving this virtual virginity, along with the fear of losing it one day.

Is the fantasm of virginity universal?

I think so, to the very point of affirming that *all women are virgins* and that the degree to which they are sexually fulfilled does not matter. Some sexually active women perceive this fantasm as a result of a particular capacity for introspection. Others, less sensitive to internal sensations and possibly less imaginative, finally feel this impression of virginity again and speak of it when they find a good listener.

Nevertheless, I encounter patients who have nothing to do with this fantasm and for whom femininity seems marked by a strong masculine identification with the father. These are women with a substantial social life and a reduced sexual activity. It is as if their imaginary virginity has given way to an ideal form of action and conquest.

And actual virginity? Do you believe that the loss of virginity is always an important event in the life of the adolescent girl?

Certainly, the loss of virginity has been considered as a major experience, a test or even a rite of passage in becoming a woman. As a result of the liberation of moral standards of the last few decades the loss of virginity is not as dramatic as it once was. Yet, girls and boys still fear their first sexual relation.

The attitude of today's adolescent with respect to the loss of virginity varies according to their personalities and their social milieu. The choices for young girls in our time are to remain a virgin until marriage while having amorous relationships that are more or less chaste, or to renounce their virginity in order to experience their sexual freedom.

And for man, what does the loss of the woman's virginity represent?

Recall that the loss of virginity was considered by certain primitive peoples to be a cursed gesture, a religious taboo. The fiancé feared being the first to break the hymen of his future wife and so the practice was confided to the care of a third party. Deflowering [*déflorer*] a young woman signified transgressing a prohibition of the gods. It was sacrilege that forecast bad luck and cataclysm. Nowadays, myths have changed. To deflower a young woman can be experienced by a man as the conquest of a trophy and the affirmation of his virility. Nevertheless, when he learns that he is the first to penetrate his partner, he is often afraid.

Afraid of what?
Afraid of either harming the girl or doing himself harm. Do not forget that fear of the unknown still exists.

The boy is afraid, even if he has the desire to be the initiator?
The feeling of triumph to be the first comes only after having accomplished the act, once he has understood that he was the agent. But, very often, young men are unaware, prior to the act, that the girl was a virgin—young women hide it often. Whatever the case may be, boys behave awkwardly with fear and haste.

And how does the young man's first experience affect him?
It is experienced as a true test of his becoming a man. Following the example of the girl, the first sexual relation represents for him a victory over his family's hold on him, that which confers upon him the status of being an adult. Nevertheless, do not overlook the fact that this major event is often a failure as confirmed by numerous testimonies of disappointed young girls. Three-fourths of young women report frustration with a first experience that is off-putting, insipid, or painful.

Is the loss of virginity always painful?
Not really. The loss of virginity is rather painless especially if the young girl desires it, is relaxed and is comfortable with her partner. Still, even so, the first relation can prove to be disappointing. The problem is not simply one of losing her virginity, but rather the fear the girl has toward the act, the guilt of having done it, or the frustration of not having attained the anticipated pleasure. If there is pain, it is caused by the young girl's anxiety.

Is it inevitable that it be so?
I think so, and the inexperience of the partners is the cause. The boy is often impatient, awkward, and ignorant of the importance

of tender gestures to awaken the desire in his partner; and the girl, when she is inexperienced, is generally indecisive, tense, and full of apprehension.

Let's not lose sight that men as often as women—above all youth—are ignorant about the morphology of the vagina. It seems that we can represent the penis or the clitoris—parts that protrude from the body—more easily than the vaginal cavity. Taken together, it seems that we have more difficulty with the mental representation of a crevice than we do a protuberance, such as the breast, clitoris, or penis. There is a stark contrast between our imagination of the vagina as opposed to a protuberance. We have generally a vague and imprecise idea of a hole but are immediately and strongly affected by any corporeal protuberance. We know not how to define the hole, but we can describe easily an appendage. I am convinced that the comportment of men is in large part determined by the fact that their sex is apparent while the comportment of women is determined by the fact that their sex is retracted. While virility is attributed to the feeling that the penis is an appendage that is vulnerable and exposed to danger, femininity is nourished by the feeling that the vagina is sheltered by the body and is inseparable from it. I will express this in another way. The virile behavior is animated by the fantasy that man says to himself thinking of his penis, "I am proud to have it but because it is so precious to me I fear losing it." Feminine behavior on the other hand is animated by the fantasy where the woman thinking of her sexuality says to herself, "My sex is very deep in my being, to desire me is to desire me whole, and not to desire me is to abandon me."

We will add that the vaginal anatomy, barely visible and misunderstood, incites a number of fantastical interpretations, in men as well as in women.

What interpretations?

Men, for example, imagine the vaginal cavity as an open hole, while in reality the vagina is folded and rather closed in on itself, with a shorter anterior side against a longer posterior side. During sex, these walls distend and adapt to the penis whatever its size may be. This power of dilation is considerable enough to permit the passage of a baby during childbirth. In sum, the vagina is not as many men think a passive receptacle for the penis; it is an active organ of feminine pleasure, a flattened cavity of walls that are extendable and excitable.

Among masculine phobias, we find often that of the "vagina-trap" in which men have fear that their sex will never be released; or there is the terror of certain patients of whom the erection is inhibited by the strange idea that their penis will be crushed against the wall that seals the vaginal orifice; and we have yet to mention the well-known legend of the "vagina dentata," a vagina that is capable of biting and chewing on the sex of he who risks penetration.

One last question. What is the parents' attitude concerning their daughter's virginity?
In an attempt to respond to your question, I would like to refer you to René Char's poem "The Schoolgirl's Companion."[5] It is a moving exchange between a father and his daughter who is on the verge of becoming a woman. First, there are the words of the father who is shaking at the thought of that his daughter will lose her innocence. His words are followed by the exalted response of the young woman.

HATE AND FRIENDSHIP

‗‗‗‗‗‗‗‗‗‗‗‗‗‗‗‗‗‗‗‗‗‗‗‗‗‗‗‗‗‗‗‗‗‗‗‗‗

HATE AS AN EVERYDAY PHENOMENON

Can we hope that some day humanity will be able to eradicate violence?

The idea that hate, war, and destruction in general can disappear is, I fear, utterly utopian. Of course, we can try to thwart violent tendencies, but don't forget that destructive forces are so inherent to human nature that they remain ineradicable. In order to better confront violence, it is essential to fight it while understanding that it will never be eliminated. Violence, like weeds, will come up again.

Hate is therefore an invincible enemy?

Most likely so, because this enemy is within us. Wherever there are human beings, hate will be found, even among the best of us. If you suppress your hate you will end up mutilating yourself, because it is a large part of you. If, for example, we deprive a child of all his aggression, we would see the child weaken into indifference and apathy, as an autistic child. You see, the health of an individual results from the equilibrium between two great contrary movements: the forces of death and those of life. While the death drive manifests itself in hate, the life drive generates love. Therefore, attraction and repulsion, love and hate, are the fundamental forces that pulsate in all that lives. Hence, it is impossible to remove a part of ourselves as essential as hate; at most, we can try to master it.

Here is my idea: a wild beast, for example, ceases to be dangerous when it is submitted to regular training. Likewise, hate needs a daily regime. I repeat: hate must be exercised everyday! But do not misunderstand me; my statement is in no way an apology for violence. On the contrary, it is a call for temperance, for if you let violence accumulate in your psyche, it will become explosive. But if it is released regularly, it becomes civilized and transforms itself into fertile energy. Psychoanalysis teaches us that the drives ferment and boil over from the pressure of a brutal repression, while they could be sublimated if simply incrementally released. I insist that hate should be constantly distilled in order to avoid, having been confined for too long in the unconscious, a violent explosion of anger. For example, if hate is expressed during a lover's spat when the partners express their anger freely, the hate will become healthier, and, when associated with love, will consolidate the relationship. Thus, the storms that sometimes destabilize a couple may also serve as a sort of safety valve for the release of excess tension. Lovers know, even if they have forgotten it in the heat of the argument, that their clash not only will not separate them, but on the contrary will solidify their relationship more than ever. Finally, domesticated hate is an excellent complement to love, which in turn it nourishes and fortifies.

I thought that hate kills love and that they have always been sworn enemies.
It is rather more like a sibling rivalry. While rivals, they belong to the same family, the family of loving and formidable chimeras. For what is love if not a delicious mirage; the illusory promise to live with another in mutual happiness? And what is hate if not the threat of an equally utopian idea of one day succeeding at destroying the other? Regarding romantic illusion, I always think of Lacan's well-known paradox, "Love is to give that which one does not have."[1] Which I would translate as, "Love is to promise the moon." Or, love is nothing but a promise of happiness always to come. This is why I tell myself that the person who is in love is, in the end, a sincere peddler of illusions who, without malice, exchanges the mirages of one for the mirages of another. But do not be mistaken, to define love as an exchange of lures is not pejorative. On the contrary, romantic innocence is, of all of our regressions, the most necessary for the survival of the species. The proof of this is that this marketplace of illusions, this exchange of nothing produces very real people like you and me. I say "children of love" independently of the authenticity of the passion that united our parents. Whatever were their feelings, it is undeniable that the fruitful sexual act always expresses the mutual desire to create life. Beyond their consciousness and their love, two beings who procreate are necessarily obeying the supreme will of the species to perpetuate itself.

Hate is also an illusion if we see it as a threat, that is to say, as the blind will to annihilate the other. In general, I will tell you that if love is the promise of infinite happiness, then hate is the threat of an absolute unhappiness. Whether we give in to love or to hate, we are always duped by an illusion; be it fulfilling the one we love or destroying the one whom we hate.

That being the case, these opposing mirages are so intertwined that they never appear without the other, to the point that their union was amusingly referred to by Lacan as *l'hainamoration* or a "hateloving." Let there be no doubt—behind the noblest of love lurks the most pernicious hate.

To return now to your question about the insurmountable nature of violence, I will repeat that far from eliminating hate we must tame it and train it to be an ally of love, and more broadly, to be a vital force that is necessary for the individual and society.

Are you saying that hate can be a beneficial energy if one is able to channel it? However, can we always succeed in doing so?
No, precisely not. I distinguish between two types of hate.[2] The first is a brute force that we can domesticate and render positive by exercising it every day. This is the *sublimated hate*, which I have already mentioned. The second form is *impulsive hate*, a destructive passion that is released when pride is attacked at its core. I am thinking of the case of a betrayed spouse who is humiliated and screams out her pain while kicking out the man she so loved. Certainly the most idealized companion is also the one whose betrayal is least forgivable. One should know that the most extreme battles are always waged by those who had the most passionate love. We should not have any doubt about it; there is no worse hate than familial hate. This is yet again a new confirmation of the strict solidarity between love and hate, these twin sisters: when one loosens its grip the other just as quickly takes hold.

But what is this *impulsive hate*? There was a news story of a raging father, who, having learned of the rape of his adolescent daughter, took his gun and killed the rapist on the spot. What fury armed the vengeful hands if not visceral hate? And what had inflamed such a flood of violence if not the pain of seeing violated something he held dear, his daughter's innocence. And yet, we all have a treasure as sacred as the purity of his child is for a father, namely, the intimate feeling of being oneself. Henceforth, to wound this deep feeling is to strike our ego at its core and unleash the fury of rage. We will thus define *impulsive hate* as an instinctive reaction of the ego, a desperate reflex that bandages the image of the injured self and calms the pain of the affront. This means that my hatred is concentrated violence against the one who has humiliated me and by humiliating me has destabilized the foundation of my identity. I would like to defile them as they had defiled me and what I held most precious: the image of myself. To hate the other is thus the ultimate reaction that attempts to repair the humiliated self-image.

That being the case, we could suppose that, as victims of an attack, we would be crushed. And yet, the response to the insult is never a collapse but hate. *I prefer to hate than be sad because in my hate I gather myself together but when I am sad I fall apart. In a word, I hate, therefore I am.*

If I understood, even blind hate fortifies us?
No, I do not think so. The feeling of omnipotence that accompanies the explosion of hatred is nothing but a nervous tension of the ego, an illusory sensation of gathering yourself. I just told you that subli-mated hate consolidates us; I will tell you now that impulsive hate weakens us. It is like a poison that eats at us and eternally shackles us to what we want to destroy. Let's look again at the example of the betrayed spouse and listen to her: "*Before being humiliated, I was dependent on him because I was in love, now I am dependent on him because I hate him. As long as he is on this earth, I will keep him from living. He must suffer as he has made me suffer.*" Such a fury demon-strates how the one who hates can be made sick by her hate and fall under the yoke of the obsessive image of the betrayer. To help you better understand the nature of this unhealthy dependence on the hated other, I suggest that you see this dependence as being just as morbid as that of the mourner who thinks the departed is still alive. Whether it is the hater haunted by the phantom of the traitor or the mourner haunted by the phantom of the departed, neither can suc-ceed at chasing the demons. One is a slave to rancor and the other to sadness, and each is oppressed by a spectral presence that devours his or her existence. Rancor and pain are often those internal fires

that we stoke, even if they undermine us to the point of rendering us physically ill.

And how does one liberate oneself from this prison that is chronic hate?

With the help of time. Gradually, one must let anger pour out, in tears, blood and sweat, and in symbols, until it dissipates. Only time, and in certain cases, the attention of a psychoanalyst, will allow the subject to open up to new emotional bonds or relationships that will progressively dissipate the nightmares of the past.

You said that hate is "the manifestation of the death drive," but what does the death drive mean to you?

At the risk of surprising you, I consider that the life drive and the death drive are both at the service of life, each in opposition to the other. The first unites and the second separates, but both work together to keep us alive as long as possible. The first—*Eros*—is the tendency that causes us to form durable bonds with others and with things. The stability that results is indispensable, for it consolidates our physical and our psychical unity and solidifies our self-image. The second, the death drive—*Thanatos*—is a power of undoing and of destruction of all that is harmful or obsolete, whether in our mind or in our body. For me, the death drive is a positive and salutary impulse that, in spite of the sinister word *death*, has the positive effect of clearing a path for us. In the realm of the mind, it is thanks to this beneficial force that we succeed at forgetting unpleasant facts and ignore those who are unpleasant to us. In the realm of the body, the death drive is equally purifying when, for example, it mobilizes the antibodies when we are sick and it brings the infant to detach herself naturally from the nursing mother during weaning. Finally, the death drive guides our choices throughout our lives. We constantly choose, and never cease to leave a thousand possible options behind us. The path that we are journeying on in time is strewn with the debris of our embryonic loves and of all that we could have become. In brief, the death drive is at work every time that in order to go on we must fend off threats, and defend ourselves from aggression, renounce that which we must naturally leave, and choose finally our destiny.

To conclude, whether it is the unifying life or the death drive that destroys externally or purifies internally, the conjoined action of the two antagonistic forces serves the cause of life.

A FRIEND IS SOMEONE WITH WHOM
I FEEL HAPPY TO BE MYSELF

How can one define friendship?
I will tell you that friendship is one of the most beautiful forms of love, for nothing is more vivifying than a true friendship. Earlier, I was explaining that romantic love is an illusion, the often joyous, at times tumultuous expectation of a happiness to come. Recall the formula: love is to promise the other that which you do not have, and to expect of him or her that which he or she does not have.

However, a love between friends is quite different. We love the friend, not for what he does not have, but for what he is, what he does have, or for what he does, and this is what makes us happy. This is why I would claim that while the amorous bond is nourished by hope, the bond of friendship is nourished by presence. While love is the expectation of an impossible gift from the lover, friendship is the welcome of an actual gift from the friend.

Among the many differences between romantic and friendly love, three of these differences seem to be essential. First, friendship connects me intimately to a man or a woman in a relationship in which sex does not play a role. Certainly, the body of my friend is sometimes the object of a lively affection, when, for example, after a long absence, I embrace the friend in an affectionate hug. But this gesture of spontaneous tenderness is in no way ambiguous, and remains devoid of any eroticism. The other difference with romantic love involves the reciprocity of feeling. I can be in love without being loved in return, but I cannot pretend to be the friend of a person who ignores me. Said another way, friendship is always a mutual feeling, in good times and bad. A final distinction: friendship is hardly possessive; my friend can see other friends without our relationship being threatened. And even if a secret jealousy insinuates itself between us, it is rarely of a passionate nature.

It seems as if friendship is approached only in relation to love?
This is true, but only as an initial characterization that allows one to see clearly the three characteristics that are proper to the bond of friendship: it is nonerotic, it is reciprocal and it is nonexclusive.

So what can we say about friendship in itself?
That it is a joy! It is a serene joy to be friends with someone who shares the same feeling. A real friend loves you just as you are, and reciprocally, you are equally happy with your friend for who he or she is. What is a friend if not the person with whom you can communicate the most intense sensation of being, that of being yourself? Obviously, this close connection that is often unexpressed can only develop over time with the constancy of feelings. As such, there is no solid friendship except the one that is progressively woven through the years, and having survived the inevitable drifting apart, crises, and conflicts of existence. In general, the ties of friendship need time to strengthen, even if, sometimes, it begins in an instant. In most cases, friendship is born from chance, and grows gradually over time until one day we are all surprised and happy to discover that the other is part of our intimate circle of friends.

I will add that an authentic friend is one who is always there when I reach out and who gives me tacit assurance that I am not alone. The best gift that you can receive from a friend, beyond his or her availability, is the intensity of his or her presence—a presence that symbolizes your engagement in the world.

What do you think of those who frequently change friends?
I think that they have missed the happiness of crafting a friendship. They do not know the pleasure of constructing a relationship that is durable and watching it grow. Customarily, we try to keep our friends as long as possible, as we have a tendency to guard the relations that help and stabilize us. As much as the discovery of something new excites us, so too, the conservation of a friendship can calm and relax us. In psychoanalysis, we often say that attraction for the already known is a thousand times stronger than the call of the new. Why? Essentially, it is because we seek peace of mind and a definitive stability. Indeed, one of the first steps in our search for stability is to instinctively protect our affective relationships, and to draw from

them an indefinable feeling of continuity. Of course, we are always evolving, but apart from the passage of time, we want to regularly confirm that we are always the same, and that our identity remains unchanged. Nothing is more reassuring!

And yet you can say that those who often change friends do not share this conservative tendency that is common to human nature. Whether by inclination or infatuation, fickle people refuse the unique experience of a secure relationship based on the intimate agreement of two sensibilities.

But why are the fickle vain in this way?

To tell you the truth, it is more than vanity; it is a question of escape. The fickle refuse to be attached out of fear of being dominated, or, on the contrary, of being abandoned by the other. Fearful, they prefer to anticipate the separation rather than risk being subjected to it, and they reject the friend before they can be rejected. On the contrary, even through faithful friends go through crises in their friendship, they have an abiding trust that gives them the sweetest of pleasures, never having to worry.

And you, how do you choose your friends?

I let myself be guided by my intuition and, in general, it works for me. This is why today I am fortunate to be able to count on old friends who support me in what I do and who I am. It means everything to receive support for one's self-image. Often on this topic, I think of a saying I coined and that has guided me for a long time: "A *friend is someone with whom I am happy to be myself.*"

That being the case, I do not deny that, in a circle of friends, there are always those who make us doubt ourselves, and those who encourage us. And this difference is essential, because we are naturally inclined to favor all that enhances our narcissistic self-image. Therefore, certain friends make us feel good insofar as they stimulate self-love, while others make us feel badly because they weaken us. It happens nonetheless that by fear of solitude or by cowardice, some people—and I have sometimes suffered from this myself—accept a friend who shows disdain for them, when they should have tried to get away from them as quickly as possible. You now understand why friendship can also be defined as the bond in which love for the other and love of self converge. When the other wishes for me what is good for me, it is the ultimate sign of real friendship.

I do not want to conclude without recalling how the great friendships of the past have influenced our destiny. Try this experiment: think of the faces of your best friends from your youth—boys and girls; reflect on them and you will find that they played a role in your important decisions; one such friend had introduced me to the person who became my wife, another introduced me to *The Interpretation of Dreams*, and with that one I have shared the pleasure of thinking. This is what friendship is: a dual awakening. Each person leads the other to discover unsuspected riches within themselves.

ANALYSIS WITH A CHILD

HOW DOES ONE SPEAK FRANKLY WITH ONE'S CHILD?

Let us talk now about children. What advice can you give to parents to improve communication with their children?
I will begin by saying the first communication with the child takes place well before birth. For the parents, the desire for the child's arrival, to be happy to feel the movement in the womb of the mother, and to be even happier to see the child being born, is already a communication with the child and a welcome into the world.

The most useful advice I can give to parents who desire to have better dialogue with their child, is to address him or her as I am addressing you right now, that is to say, by taking the child to be a real part of the discussion. One must realize that the child, as small as he or she is, fully perceives our intentions. So we ought to speak with the child with the firm conviction that he or she understands what we say. A newborn, for example, does not grasp the meaning of our sentences, but intuitively captures the essence of our message.

But how does one with speak with a child concretely?
It is crucial to look directly into the eyes when speaking to a child, using authentic language that comes from the heart. If the mother is from a country other than France, she should not hesitate to talk with the child in her native language, as children are not disturbed by a mixing of cultures.

One must also choose the most favorable moment to tell the child about important things. It is not necessary to make long speeches! On the contrary, one should use few words, and speak clearly. I emphasize that, when talking with a child, adults should be convinced that the child is able to understand what one is saying. It is an essential condition of all productive dialogue. We know that the most beautiful expressions serve no purpose if they are said without the expectation that the other will be touched. If a father is certain

55

of being understood by his son, the inflection of his voice and the melody of his phrases will strike the right chord in the soul of his son. When a mother, in the morning, takes her baby to day care and says, "I must go to work now, Ms. Annette will take care of you and I will be back to get you this afternoon at five o'clock," she gives the child a clear message, which is true and reassuring; reassuring because the mother leaves her child with peace of mind.

That is a model parent! But what does the child feel when separated from the mother all day?
The child suffers, it is indisputable, but if the separation is accompanied by the right words, as did this mother who took the time to explain to the child the new situation, the suffering disappears, and in its place is a feeling of security that assures the infant until the next developmental crisis when he or she will again leave the known to confront the unknown. This is when it will become necessary way to accompany the child through this delicate passage, like all those to come, and explain to him or her the difficulties and the satisfactions that await.

And what about mothers who do not know how to talk to their children?
All mothers know how to talk! That is, all of the mothers who are happy to be mothers. The problem is not one of knowing what to say, but of being soothing in the words that are said; the problem does not come from the words, but in the manner in which they are said. The force of a word does not reside in the meaning it conveys but in the emotion that animates it; it is never the verb that signifies but the presence that emanates from it. In short, words remain the most useful buffer in a difficult situation, under the condition that they are sincere.

SEVEN CRISES THAT A CHILD ENDURES
IN ORDER TO GROW UP

You have spoken of "developmental crises." What do you mean by "crises?"
The physiological, psychological, and social development of a child does not follow a uniform line but progresses in sporadic surges, each one a developmental crisis. With each crisis, the child departs from the known to confront the unknown; the child leaves a comfort-

able state that is no longer age-appropriate in order to launch new abilities, whether it is in the domain of emotions, intellect, motility, or sociability. As such, each crisis is a leap ahead, a leap from an outdated state toward a new one. Obviously, each child progresses, stabilizes, and sometimes even regresses, according to his or her own pace. For example, a child could momentarily refuse to use the toilet even after toilet training, because the child prefers to stay in the crib and remain an infant.

It is a regression?

Yes, a healthy and necessary regression that the parents should respect. A child who regresses, who refuses to get through something difficult, is a child who does not feel ready to go forward. The best way of helping is to accept the setback rather than to force the child to grow up. When the moment arrives, you can be sure that the child will be where he or she needs to be, especially if he or she knows that his or her parents understand him or her and are not impatient to see the child progress.

For a child, maturation involves the recurring experience of loss and gain: loss of the security of yesterday and gain of the security of today. One could simplify it by saying that all developmental crises entail two facets, that which the child loses and that which the child gains: *That which the child abandons* and *that which the child acquires*.

However, to these two movements of renunciation and acquisition, one must add that of the sedimentation of acquisitions, since maturing also involves the accumulation of rewards from the different challenges that have been overcome. Therefore, beyond that which is lost and gained, there is *that which the child holds on to forever*. This is how the personality is formed. I would like to say that all developmental crises are composed of three simultaneous movements: *renouncing* the prior state, *acquiring* the future state, and *reaping* the best of the past. In other words, the child grows up while painfully detaching itself from the people and the things that belong to the past, while overcoming itself, and conserving its essential acquisitions.

Chronologically, what are the principal crises that a child must face?

If you consider the period that goes from birth to the end of adolescence, we can list seven crises that the child must pass through to enter adulthood. I call them the "*Seven crises that a child endures in order to grow up,*" each one a rung on the ladder of the stages of life. In chronological order, the crises are:

Birth
Weaning (from 3 to 6 months old)
Discovery of walking and of language (from 1 to 3 years old)
First schooling (between 2 and 5 years old)
Discovery of an inner life (toward 6/7 years old)
First love outside of the family (between 13 and 15 years old)
Leaving home (between 18 and 25 years old)

You will recall that each of these crises has three components: *That which the child leaves behind; that which he or she acquires; and that which he or she will hold on to forever.*

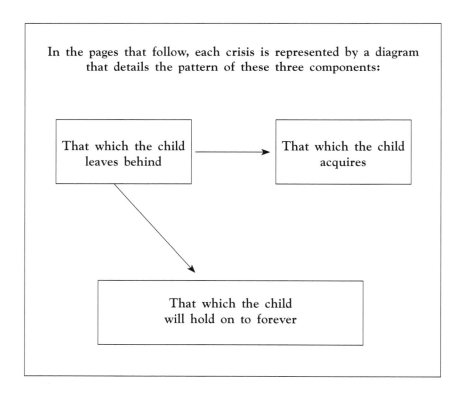

1. Birth

That which the child leaves behind

The passive and symbiotic state of life as a fetus

That which the child acquires

The active and desiring state of life outside the womb

That which the child will hold on to forever

The desire and pleasure of sleeping.
The elementary sensation of being alive.

2. Weaning (from 3 to 6 months old)

That which the child leaves behind

- The breast of the mother experienced by the child as a part of him or herself.
- The primacy of the mouth (sucking) for experiencing the world.

That which the child acquires

- The aptitude of nourishing oneself with increasingly solid foods that are perceived by the child as things distinct from him or herself.
- The mouth and the throat, vocal organs for language: infantile speech and babbling.

That which the child will hold on to forever

The desire and pleasure of sucking.

3. Discovery of walking and of language (from 1 to 3 years old)

That which the child leaves behind

- Moving on all fours.
- Babbling.
- The feeling of non-differentiation between oneself and others
- The private world of the mother-child couple.

That which the child acquires

- Walking that allows the child to be near or far from the mother.
- The first sentences, the first, "No!" and the first "I Want!"
- Ability to control the sphincter and the pride of mastering the body.
- Awareness of the difference between the self and others.
- The perception of the mother as independent from the child.
- The recognition of the father as a person who is different than the mother.

That which the child will hold on to forever
The desire and pleasure of being in a couple.

4. First schooling (between 2 and 5 years old)

That which the child leaves behind

- The reassuring family nest.
- The idea that the father and mother are of the same sex.

That which the child acquires

- The first interactions outside of the family. The first crushes. The sense of friendship.
- The idea that the father is a man and that the mother is a woman.
- Desire as a girl or as boy.

That which the child will hold on to forever

The sense of family.

5. Discovery of an inner life (toward 6/7 years old)

That which the child leaves behind

- The conviction that his or her parents know all of his or her thoughts.
- Infantile immodesty and innocence.

That which the child acquires

- The age of reason and consciousness of death.
- The discovery of an inner life. First secrets and first lies.
- Modesty, shame, and guilt
- The pleasure of day dreams.

That which the child will hold on to forever

Innocence, the pleasure of confiding with the other in complete confidence, and the desire to share one's thoughts and emotions.

6. First love outside of the family (between 13 and 15 years old)

That which the child leaves behind

- Exclusive familial love.

That which the adolescent acquires

- The love of a partner selected outside of the family.
- The discovery of sexuality and the affirmation of his or her sexual identity.

That which the adolescent will hold on to forever

The indelible imprint of the attachment to his or her parents (love-hate).

7. Leaving home (the end of adolescence and the beginning of life as an adult) —between 18 and 25 years old—

That which the youth leaves behind

- The world of childhood and adolescence.

That which the young adult acquires

- Material autonomy.
- Social ideals and projects.
- Interest in making an effort and in challenging oneself.
- The capacity for compromise.

That which the young adult holds on to forever

The child in the adult, the thirst to learn, the pleasure of creating, the joys of friendship and the ability to think critically.

FLORENT AND LOUISE: THE FIRST MEETING
OF A CHILD WITH A PSYCHOANALYST

Still on the subject of children, for which sorts of problems do you generally see children in your practice?
It varies greatly but currently the most common motives that bring parents to call a psychoanalyst are for issues with slow language development, problems in school, phobias, trouble with sleep and eating, and bedwetting, as well as aggressive and choleric behavior.

I would like to clarify right away that with some children it is not always necessary to get them into therapy. For example, one does not need to consult a therapist because a four-year-old boy is incontinent. At that age, incontinence is a regressive phase and it would be excessive to speak of it as bedwetting. Let's be clear, the analysis of a child is a serious undertaking that should not be entered into casually. It would be better to exercise prudence before recommending analysis. It is only after a second or third interview that I can conclude if therapy is necessary or not. If, in the end, analysis is recommended, I will do all that is possible so that it will be of the shortest possible duration.

What if the child refuses to go to the appointments?
That rarely occurs. But when a child does not want to be engaged, I make it a rule to never force him or her. Forcing attendance at appointments would be an error because starting therapy without the full will of the patient will result in failure. The young patient should be quite motivated in order to begin the treatment. Nevertheless, it can happen that a child is reticent on arrival, but then will leave the first meeting with a desire to return.

I suppose that you do not have the children lie down on the couch during the sessions?
No, of course not! I do not use the couch except for adults and certain adolescents, and never at the beginning of treatment. I welcome the child around a little table, an actual workspace for the juvenile unconscious. With the child, I use all of the possible means of communication, including drawing, painting, molding clay, and figurines, and, of course, gestures and speech.

I would like to discuss a particularity in my manner of welcoming the young patient during the first visit. In fact, at the first interview, I never allow the parents to enter before having first seen the child alone. Contrary to common practice, I prefer to receive the child first, and only after twenty minutes alone do I go to the waiting room and invite the parents to join us. After the first few meetings with the child, I will invite the mother and then the father separately once or twice, and then, at the end of the treatment, I receive the entire family together for a last time in order to offer an assessment of the work accomplished.

And why see the child without the parents?
For many reasons, including the fact that I like the child to feel privileged and sense that he or she holds the key to the problem. I also know from experience that the first moment of the first meeting with a child, and in general with any other patient, is an important one because of the powerful force of first impressions. The initial impact is always the most penetrating and indelible. I cannot tell you how many times at the end of the treatment I have been moved to hear the analysand say the very same words that they uttered at the beginning, when so many things have changed in the meantime! Believe me, the first meeting is, for the practitioner, an exceptional moment that is not to be missed, because it contains the seed of most of what will emerge later.

On the subject of first impressions, a question has hounded me for a long time. Why are some of us so sensitive to things that are new? What is there in the first contact that exhilarates us, makes us anxious, and makes us so susceptible to others? I am of the opinion that the excitement of beginnings can only be explained by the taste for surprise and the desire for eternal youth. Each new relation is at heart a new birth, and *a fortiori* the first meeting is as well. Nothing is more vivifying than the freshness of a first meeting when the patient approaches the unknown alone and the therapist is open to the unexpected. Each of them gathers up his or her past and offers at the first moment of the encounter a new and virginal gesture. In this way, two innocents seal their union: the honesty of a subject who opens up, and the curiosity of an analyst who has everything to learn. The one who asks to be understood is as honest as the one who is prepared to listen.

You understand now why I prefer to disregard everything I had heard about the child when I see him or her for the first time. When a mother calls me to make an appointment, I never investigate the reason for the consultation. I do attach much significance to the telephone call, because it allows me to prepare for the first meeting. After setting up an appointment, I make clear to the mother that when the child asks her about the reason for the appointment, she should respond spontaneously with what she is thinking. I counsel her to also make clear that she has "called Doctor Nasio," while recommending that she pronounce my name clearly so the child may recall it. I ask her to remind the child of my name and of the date of the appointment two or three times in the preceding week, and in particular the night before. You can imagine that by so addressing myself to the mother, I inspire confidence not only in her, but in the father and in the child as well. The only things that a psychoanalyst can offer by telephone are simple directives that can give the mother reassurance that her child is already being taken care of. As for the child, knowing the name of the psychoanalyst before having met creates a direct entrance into the transference. For a child—and for all patients in general—the name of the psychoanalyst is fundamental. I consider that the transference is an emotional attachment to the therapist that occurs straightaway with the impact of his or her name. When one consults a psychoanalyst, one must know that the analyst's name is the first transferential anchorage. Transference, we can say, is the love of a name.

Practically speaking, how do you handle the first meeting with a child?
I go into the waiting room, greet the parents, and then I speak directly to the child. For example, to a young girl of three or four years, I will say, "Hello, Louise. Please come in." Invariably, her parents will rise to accompany her, but I intervene just as quickly and say, "One moment, please. I would like to see Louise first and then I will see you." Confronted with a direct invitation, the child will hesitate, then accept timidly and follow me. Once in the office, without closing the door, I show her the room where I work, the little table where we will seat ourselves, the stool where she will take her seat and the two chairs for the parents. I will sit in my chair at first and ask a still hesitant Louise to shut the door behind her. Finally,

she will make her way to the little table on which I have arranged some paper, markers, modeling clay, and a box containing a variety of objects such as safety scissors, a whistle, marbles, a mirror, shells, etc.

I then invite Louise to sit, and knowing nothing of her story, ask: "Do you know my name?"

Sometimes the child will shake her head "No." I will then introduce myself, "I am Doctor Nasio," writing my name so that she can read it, even if she does not know yet how to read or spell.

I also request that she write her own name for me. I then ask her, "Do you know what I do?" She will most likely respond that she does not, so I respond, "I see children like you, sometimes older children, occasionally infants or grownups who all come to see me to tell me about their worries. Do you know what a worry is?"

Often, the answers are surprising. I recall a three-year-old child responded quite simply, "I have a cold…!" And I, amused, smiled and told him that I was not a doctor of colds but a "doctor of worries." After having explained that a worry is what we have when we cry, when we are not happy, or when we are scared, I added, "And you, what is your worry? Why are you coming to see me?"

It is in this way that I begin the first encounter with a child patient.

And then what happens?

I would like to respond by telling you about a particular case, that of Florent, an eight-year-old boy who was referred to me for sleeping problems. During our first interview, I asked him what he thought about when he could not fall asleep, and if he was bothered by dark thoughts. He told me no, and immediately, to my surprise, he broke down crying. After a short silence, I asked him: "Why are you crying?" And he answered curiously by showing me his cheek and saying: "I'm hurt here." I then asked, "What happened to you?" "Marc and Karim hit me yesterday at the playground," he said.

Gradually, I discovered that Florent was a depressed child, bullied by his classmates, terrorized each morning by the idea of going to school. In truth, the insomnia was nothing but a secondary manifestation of his sadness. After this revealing discussion, I concluded the first part of the session by sharing my impressions with him: "Florent, your problem isn't one of sleep, but rather the fear of being beaten by the boys who do not like you. That's what makes you sad. So, the first decision to make is to change schools and, if you want to, you can come and talk to me until you feel better. Now, I will invite your father and your mother to come in and I will ask: 'Florent has just explained to me why he wanted to see me, and why do you think he should have come to see me?'" I then continue to address the child directly, "We will see what your parents will say…" This creates a complicity between the child and I myself and with it we stand before the parents as allies, together, awaiting the response from the parents.

I will then bring the parents in from the waiting room as I said I would. Still in Florent's presence, I inquire as to the reason for their visit. They respond that their child's problem is related to trouble sleeping, compounded by excessive timidity. Their answer never contains the real causes of the child's suffering, namely, the terror of being beaten, loss of self-esteem, and the anxiety at school. At the end of the interview, I share with them my conclusions and have an agreement with Florent regarding the necessity of beginning treatment.

And the analysis with the child ended well?
Yes, it was very positive. Florent had not only recovered a healthy sleeping pattern, but he also felt comfortable with his new friends at his new school. His treatment, which lasted six months, was marked by a decisive session. Florent made a drawing that symbolized the cause of his sadness. It was of a person with a huge mean face and enormous hands, holding on a leash a little dog that looked miserable. This image made me realize immediately that Florent perceived life through the prism of an unconscious feeling of humiliation. I revealed this feeling to him while commenting on his drawing with words that were accessible to him.

You should be aware that children who are beaten—even if it is only occasionally—draw figures with hands disproportionately large and strong. This is the way that the unconscious of a beaten child subtly guides the crayon to enlarge the hands, that is to say, the part of the body of another that is the most charged with affect.

Let me say at the outset that after this drawing session Laurent felt better, and the treatment entered a final phase. What had happened? Why had the symptoms disappeared? The child made the drawing just after I had told him the details of a conversation I had with his father the day before. Among other things, I told him that his father regretted having sometimes slapped him. I added that I had perceived the degree to which his father had been demanding and how he, Florent, must have felt small before him. It was at that time, without saying a word, that he began drawing the figure with the small dog.

Why had you thought the picture expressed humiliation?

Not only humiliation, but also, as strange as it might seem, the *pleasure of humiliation*. It is this coexistence of pain and pleasure that we call the moral masochism of the neurotic, which is to take pleasure at feeling humiliated. Without a doubt, Florent at this time had a parasitic, masochistic scene in his unconscious that made him believe that he could not be loved without being belittled by another.

When looking at the two figures in the picture, the brutal master and the abused little dog, I realized that the boy had been in the grip of an unconscious scene that made him view the world as a cruel one where victims hate and love their torturer. Having identified Florent as the sad little dog in the drawing, I *felt* that this boy confused the pleasure of being loved and the pain of being victimized. I underscore the word *felt* because what I relived through identification with the character of "Florent-little dog," was the pleasure of humiliation. I heard, as it were, resonate within myself, the sobs—plaintive, and also complacent—of a humiliated Florent. Then, speaking to him about it, I had tried to verbalize in the most appropriate terms this emotion, a mixture of pleasure and pain.

What did you say to him?

I pointed out to him that the dog with the leash would have felt protected, even if his master was angry with him. He confirmed that in effect the master made him suffer, but that the dog loved him dearly all the same. Our dialogue went along in this way until Florent realized on his own how much being loved for him signified being mistreated, whether by his father or by his friends. As I said before, treatment was terminated shortly after the drawing session. I think that Florent's recognition of his ambivalent attitude had freed him from his masochistic fantasy.

I would like to add that if my intervention had some positive effects, it was because the child, when drawing, had opened the door of his unconscious, permitting me to see, in complete innocence, the graphic projection of his masochistic fantasy. It is important to realize that our patients, both children and adults, play an active part in the process of healing. Any accomplishment in treatment always involves the combined contributions of the psychoanalyst and the patient. The patient allows his or her unconscious to be revealed, the psychoanalyst apprehends it and translates it into words. You must realize that if Florent had not made that drawing, I mean if he had not represented his unconscious in an image, I would have never understood the morbid desire of this boy to let himself be humiliated in order to feel loved.

Yet my intellectual understanding of his drawing would have been incomplete without my emotional understanding. As I told you, thanks to my identification with the character, "Florent humiliated little dog" I could feel his masochistic experience and express it in words. In fact, I did not *see* the composite character "Florent humiliated little dog"—as only the dog was drawn—but *I felt in my body this character that I imagined.*

You can see the extent to which an *emotional identification* is a difficult mental feat for the psychoanalyst; it permits the experienced practitioner to perceive in him or herself the unconscious feelings of the patient. Recall our metaphor of the divers in the film *Le Grand Bleu.* For a therapist, the identification of which I am speaking does not signify putting oneself in the place of the real child sitting before him or her, but to place him or herself in the place of the child he or she imagines. What is imagined is not a personal reverie, but rather is a manifestation of all that he or she knows about the history of the young patient. To conclude, I will say that the psychoanalyst is an intermediary between the *imagined child* in his or her mind and the *real child* of the session. Therefore, I try to be the bridge between them, the messenger who narrates to the present child in the session that which I learned from the unconscious one. I always say that the psychoanalyst is the *narrator of the unconscious.*

IN PRAISE OF HARD WORK

<hr>

ALBERTINE'S CHARM

Can you now speak a bit about yourself? How did your interest in psychoanalysis begin?
I spent my youth in Argentina, submerged in a universe of medicine and books. My father was a respected gastroenterologist who had devoted his life to scientific research and writing, medical as well as literary texts. He was a humanist and a clinician who was passionate about working with his patients. I would like to tell you about a childhood memory that is dear to me. When I was no more than twelve, my father started to bring me to work with him at the hospital, on a regular basis, in order to "assist" him with his consultations. I put on the white coat and stood beside patients while they underwent examinations that were often quite unbearable. The worst was certainly an esophagoscopy. For someone who is already sick and suffering, inserting a large metal tube twenty centimeters long into the esophagus is, without a doubt, a trying experience. I recall my father, before beginning the procedure, in order to make things easier, saying to the patient: "Sir, I would like to introduce my son Juan-David, a future doctor, who will be with you today. Now, I will ask you to please relax and breathe deeply." During the intubation, I'd approach the patient and try to comfort him. Today, I see in that gesture of support the start of my life as the psychoanalyst that I would become.

A few years later, as my father foresaw, I began my medical studies. Once a doctor, I specialized in psychiatry. I then decided to go to France, with the goal of deepening my understanding of French culture and to study Lacanian psychoanalysis. I arrived in Paris in 1969 and settled there permanently.

Was that when you first encountered Lacan?
Yes, I still have a vivid memory of my first encounter with Lacan. I was young and intimidated, having difficulty speaking French, but

driven by the excitement of living a dream, and knowing at last someone, who at that time, incarnated the future of psychoanalysis. He seemed to tower over me, an imposing figure who symbolized knowledge, power, and the force to create.

What was he like?

He always made a point of taking great care with his appearance; his grey hair impeccably combed back, his white shirt always with a Maoist style collar, and his unusual suit coat, which was shiny with mauve and yellow colors. But beyond his mannered style, I could still sense the power of his gaze that was at once distant and penetrating. I particularly recall his smile of satisfaction when he discovered that I had traveled to France to attend his *École* with a fellowship granted by the French Embassy in Argentina. He was both surprised and pleased to learn the French government officially recognized his teaching to the point of financing the schooling in Paris of a young, foreign, psychiatrist.

You then became his patient?

No, I was never his patient, but rather, I was an assiduous student. I had the good fortune of seeing him in private many times throughout the year when we looked at the first Spanish edition of his *Écrits* together. He had not liked the translation and wanted a Spanish-speaking psychoanalyst who was familiar with his theories to correct it. Our meetings took place in the evenings after his consultations, in restaurants in the Seventh Arrondissement, and sometimes on Sunday mornings in his country home at Guitrancourt. I thus had the rare privilege of getting him to clarify many obscure passages in his book. I confess that in this intimate, intellectual environment, it occurred to me to deliberately ask many questions and to push him to explain a number of allusions that for the ordinary reader of *Écrits* remain enigmatic.

Later, once integrated into the community of students who were close to him, I was able to develop a more formal relationship with him. As such, over the course of seven years, I went each week to *rue de Lille* to discuss my work with patients with him.

You only spoke of your clinical activity?

No, sometimes our exchanges drifted toward a conceptual problem often tied to my practice. But whether it was about patients or about theory, I will never forget the richness of these supervisory meetings. The most unforgettable experience during those years happened on a Tuesday in May 1979. That day, I had the rare honor of being invited by Lacan to give a lecture before the large audience of his *Séminaire*, on a theme I had discussed with him a few months earlier. I had never thought his interest in my work would extend to a proposal to speak to his students. This all took place in twenty-four hours. Monday morning, he arrived at my supervisory meeting and I heard but one sentence, "Nasio, tomorrow you will have the responsibility for my seminar!" You can imagine how stunned I was! Having accepted, I left the building at *rue de Lille* and immediately canceled all of my meetings for the day in order to work without interruption on writing a text that remains, for me, the most inspired text I have ever written.[1]

On the subject of writing, how did you experience the two cultures of Argentina and France?
Like everyone else, I am the product of innumerable transplantations that after many years have forged my identity. No one can escape the supreme rule: we are all composite beings that are born "one" and die "manifold." Without a doubt, each person is an indivisible singularity, but his or her soul is plural. Personally, one of the transplantations that most affects me is the French language. It is a language that never ceases to mold me like living clay, the spirit of which passes through my thoughts, shapes my writing, and refines my listening as a psychoanalyst.

I am convinced that the fusion of two cultures is a powerful stimulant for reflection, and that bilingualism is an opportunity for those who practice it. The constant battle to appropriate an adopted tongue is an excellent exercise of disassociation and reunification of the self that makes one more flexible and more open.

What about your native language?
I live in Paris, I speak, write, and even dream in French, but the rhythm of my ideas, the intonations and vibrations of my voice are profoundly Argentinean. I would say that I am Argentinean in rhythm and French in spirit. It may be surprising, but I have often noted that the inflection and the accent of my voice determine the words I employ. I might even say, I do not think nor write except with words that I can pronounce. In fact, it is an observation that

applies to us all: we only speak or write sentences that are attuned with the tone of our voice. I often ask myself, for instance, what kind of voice must Verlaine have had in order to set his unique nostalgic melody into verse. I could likewise generalize and say that beyond the voice, we can write only those sentences that resonate in our bodies. Take the case of Spanish or Italian, languages that I speak, and you can readily see how their musicality demands a frank and direct participation of the body. Like the majority of the speakers of the Romance languages, I gesture often, and move about while talking. It has even happened that I write while walking. It was by pacing in the gardens of the Hospital of Sainte-Anne that in 1970 I wrote my first text published in French, "Metaphor and Phallus." I kept walking around a flowerbed until the words came to me. The moment it happened, I then ran up the staircase of the library to write the words on paper. I would then go down the steps just as quickly, and back to the garden in search of new inspiration. Between the library filled with the souls of our masters, and the garden where I often crossed paths with the patients, I learned to write in French and to reflect on Freud.

And today, the old master inspires you still?
Absolutely! Reading Freud remains for me an act of constant discovery and is a true pleasure, it is as if I am sitting beside him and listening to him think. When we read Freud, we understand him and think that we are unique in receiving his message. The sentences resonate so powerfully within us that they reveal who we are. There is an exceptional connection between a writer who unveils and a reader who feels laid bare. In a word, the pleasure of reading Freud is the pleasure of feeling intelligent and more lucid about oneself. It makes Freud contemporary, because his words resonate in us and make us feel alive. Freud is resolutely modern in that the relevance and astuteness of his observations push us to understand ourselves. The day that this spark is extinguished, the works of Freud will become obsolete and be nothing more than a kind of sacred, but dead, bible.

When did you hear of Freud for the first time?
Ah! I have a vivid memory of my first contact with Freudian theory. When I was a young medical student, I had passed by a packed lecture hall. Curious to know what was being said, I took a seat in the back.

I was immediately enthralled by the eloquence of the professor who was teaching psychoanalysis. It was as if a gadfly had stung me. Then, I forgot about it. Many years later, I learned that the professor had been Angel Garma, one of the greatest psychoanalysts of that time. My initial encounter with psychoanalysis was marked by the words of a teacher. And here I find myself today, a teacher...

With the same energy and drive as that professor?
I hope so! Teaching is for me a true pleasure, and this pleasure plays a decisive role in the transmission of knowledge. Everyone knows that an inspired teacher inspires others! Often my enthusiasm stimulates the student and strengthens his or her desire to learn, which in turn, reinforces my own spirit.

When I teach, I force myself to be as clear as possible, which for me is a manner of explaining to the student, that which is already inside him or her in an embryonic state. To teach with clarity is to translate the nascent idea in the students into words, make the students conscious of it, and give them the means of developing it further. This is why an idea clearly presented always gives the impression of having been evident. Think of how many times, at the end of a class with good teacher, we are happy to realize that what we have just heard, we already knew...although we didn't have the words to express it. This is the kind of clarity that we need because it brings us the happiness of understanding and encouragement to think.

Note that the art of being a professor is to open up and release the knowledge of the students, much like the psychoanalyst does when interpreting the words of his or her patient. What else could an interpretation be if not the intervention of the therapist in order to reveal the buried conflict of the patient? If teaching is to put a name on the latent knowledge of the student, psychoanalytic interpretation is to put a name on the unconscious conflict the patient suffers. In spite of their differences, you can easily admit the striking affinity between the act of teaching and the psychoanalytic act.

Beyond being clear, I'm always concerned with presenting my work in a manner that would stimulate the imagination of the audience. I try to personify the ideas and try to make them play the different roles of a scientific fiction. When I study a concept, I see its beginning, watch it grow, and open up onto other concepts, and like a character, it tells me the story of its birth, its filiations, and its history. It is in this way that I conceive of my theoretical writings: they should show the rhythm and the movements of the concept, the sudden ruptures, the twists and paradoxes. I call this type of transmission of ideas that anthropomorphizes an abstract entity and spontaneously leads the listener to appropriate it with his or her imagination, "*dramatizing a concept.*"

I realize that I am very visual in my approach to theory, and sometimes I do not hesitate to act out even the most formal ideas. I sometimes mime a difficult idea in my seminar with a gesture.

What would be an example?

Recently, when I was explaining the concept of the "splitting of the ego," I surprised myself by illustrating the concept with a gesture typical of a schizophrenic, who, in the course of a crisis of depersonalization, suffers from such a splitting. While I was speaking, I reproduced mechanically the corporeal attitude that I had seen so many times in psychotics: bringing my hand to my eyes slowly, turning it and staring at it intensely while anxiously wondering if this strange hand was really my own. The questions and the reactions of the audience confirmed that the mimicry of depersonalization had greatly enhanced their access to a concept as complex as that of the "splitting of the ego."

When working at my desk and realizing I need to dig deeper into an abstract theme, I have the same need to dramatize. Like a director, I try to dramatize the concept while creating the suspense of an intrigue that builds to a climax and then finds resolution.

What kind of intrigue?

Let us take the case of one of the more difficult notions in Jacques Lacan's theory, that of "*objet petit a.*" Concretely, what is *objet petit a*? Let us look at the following scene. A man confides in us:

"I am madly in love with Albertine."

We then ask him:

"What is it about her that you find so irresistible? Is it her physical appearance?"

"No doubt," he replies.

"Her intelligence?"

"Certainly."

"But tell me exactly, what does she mean to you?"

"She is the woman whom I love passionately!"

"Yes, but more precisely, what is it about her that attracts you to her?"

"Well, I told you that I love her body, her sensibility, her talent....Ah! I also love that she is a piano teacher..."

"And what else..." I insist.

"And so I love her....Look, I do not know why. Do not ask so many questions! I love her; that is all! There is something about her that seduces and captivates me."

That is *objet petit a*, it is that which fascinates and dazzles the lover. It is the grace that emanates from Albertine. The *objet petit a* is—in order for you to better understand me, I will use a contemporary word, that of "charm"—the charm of the loved one. But what is charm? I recall a wonderful text from Plato, the *Charmides*. It is one of the most beautiful writings of the great philosopher, in which the character Charmides intervenes, a young man whose exquisite beauty moved Socrates. When reading this text, I always think of the perplexity of the old master—so little inclined to emotion—when in contact with the tender Charmides. I imagine Socrates asking himself silently: "What is it that excites me so? Why am I so moved when this boy approaches? Is it his beauty, his quick wit, or simply his presence? What is a presence?" I say: it is charm. But what is charm? What is this spellbinding energy that emanates from a person and delights us? The enchantment is the theft of seduction, the violence of love. The lover feels suddenly snatched from him or herself, his or her liberty taken, and under the spell of the loved one. Now, how could we explain the mystery of charm? We cannot do it. To address the very difficulty, Lacan had named the magic of charm: "*objet petit a*." The *objet a* is thus the name given to the ineffable and intoxicating presence of the loved one, a presence that makes him or her irreplaceable in my heart.

In the end, what is *objet petit a*? The *objet petit a* is the essence of the loved one. It is not the *body*, nor the *image* of the loved one, not even *what he or she represents*. It is all of that and more than that. It is his or her irresistible presence that, like a whirlwind, sucks me in and carries me away. The *objet petit a* is a hollow, a lack; it is the other as a lack that inspires my desire. Whether named Charmides or Albertine, the loved one is, for the lover, the always to be conquered object.

That was an example of a small bit of improvised theater that dramatized one of the more subtle psychoanalytic notions. I hope that I was able to reveal its deep meaning, that of defining the other that we love as the lack that inspires our desire.

Can you apply the same method to a Freudian concept?
Let us try. Take the manner in which Freud conceived of the functioning of mental life. Recall that in his work, our psyche is considered to be governed by the cohabitation of two groups of antagonistic forces. One group is always striving to be externalized—they are the drives of the Id—while another group firmly opposes it—these are the tendencies of the ego, which work at censorship. You have probably seen on television a commercial that shows a man doing whatever comes to his mind: he runs through the streets, kisses an unknown woman on the mouth while she is arguing with her friend, then he takes off his clothes and plunges into a fountain. This is what someone would never dare do, unless demented: let oneself go without resisting the most primitive impulses. The savage drives are thwarted by the reasonable tendencies of the conscious ego. And yet sometimes it happens that some of the primitive drives escape the censorship while others fail and remain contained. The functioning of mental life—and it is there where I apply the technique of dramatization—can be summed up in four phases: *that which pushes, that which resists, that which goes through, and that which remains. That which pushes* are those primitive drives from the Id; *that which resists* is the barrier of repression put up by the Ego; *that which goes through* are the few primitive drives that make it past the barrier and succeed at externalizing themselves; and finally, *that which remains* are the other drives that are likewise primitive and, blocked from expression, ferment in the unconscious. Such is the war between the primitive drives and those of the ego, a war one sees every time one encounters the dynamic human psyche.

What are neuroscientists saying today about the psychoanalytic approach?
Actually, there is a surprising similarity between psychoanalysis and neuroscience. Many neuroscientific discoveries bring Freudian propositions to mind, to the extent that some researchers refer to a "neuronal unconscious," and others confirm more particularly the

mechanism of repression. I am thinking also of the neurobiologists such as J. P. Changeux and A. R. Damasio who localize in the neuron what we can call a presentation. Changeux spoke of "stock images" that he names "mental objects," and Damasio introduced the term "dispositional representation"[2] to describe the capacity of the neuron to produce a memory. The appearance of a painful memory, for example, would result from the reactivation of the potential representation. The potential representation does not designate an intra-neuronal element, but rather an inter-neuronal system that is put on hold and that waits to be reactivated. Likewise, it is surprising that Damasio had selected the word *representation*, vocabulary borrowed from psychology of the nineteenth century, taken up by Freud, and still utilized by psychoanalysts. Without getting involved in the complexity of the psychoanalytic definition of the concept "representation," an evident affinity ties the Freudian notion of unconscious representation "capable of becoming conscious"[3] and that of neurobiology with their "dispositional representation" capable of becoming a memory. Beyond the particulars of each, we are no less moved to see the father of psychoanalysis in dialogue, irrespective of time and fashion, with scientists in the twenty-first century.

What are you currently researching?
I am still taken with a proposition advanced in 1978, but which remains open to debate, that of an *eventful unconscious, produced and unique*. What does that mean? First, that the unconscious does not exist at all times. It appears only at privileged moments, for example, in treatment when singular events occur, I mean when the psychoanalyst or the patient feels an intense emotion and lets out a word or a gesture that surprises him or her. The unconscious is, as such, an eventful unconscious. That is to say, there is no unconscious before or after, but only during an event; the unconscious is intrinsic to the event. This implies, and this is the second characteristic: the unconscious is never already there, at the ready, preexisting the act; but rather, it is intrinsic to the act. It is present in a given lapse, a given dream, and in any involuntary manifestation of the patient or the psychoanalyst. Contrary to popular belief, the unconscious is not the reservoir of the soul, but a spark that ignites at critical moments in analytic discourse. The third characteristic is in regard to the remarkable mobility of the unconscious. It can originate in one

person and then manifest itself in another. I have formulated this as: *the psychoanalyst dreams aloud that which the patient represses in silence*, or more exactly, *the psychoanalyst perceives in his or her own psyche the repressed emotions of the analysand*. For this reason, I affirm that the unconscious is not individual, but shared in common between partners in analysis. There is not one unconscious proper to the psychoanalyst, on the one hand, and, another unconscious proper to the patient, on the other hand, but one *singular and unique* unconscious produced during a surprising event in a session, the incarnation of the *in-between* of the analytic encounter.

You may find contradictory this hypothesis of a *single unconscious* shared between two partners, which I formulated during our first interview, according to which the psychoanalyst—a diver of the mind—works with the instrument of *his or her own unconscious* (that which I called "instrumental unconscious"). But this contradiction is only apparent because it was first necessary that the psychoanalyst engage his or her own unconscious—instrumental unconscious— in order to create an intimate union with the unconscious of the patient. When the psychoanalyst perceives the repressed emotion of the patient with his or her unconscious and translates it into words, he or she is so immersed in the psyche of the patient that the frontier between the unconscious of the one and the unconscious of the other fades. In the final analysis, the unconscious is, for me, an *eventful agency, co-produced* by the protagonists of the psychoanalytic dialogue.

The other thesis that seems to me to contribute to a better understanding of certain symptoms that resist the therapeutic action of psychoanalysis, such as compulsive acting out, certain psychosomatic disorders, drug addiction, or even hallucination, is that of the "*Formations of jouissance*." While the manifestations of the unconscious (slips, parapraxes, dreams, etc.) can all be symbolized, that is to say, expressed in words, the manifestations or Formations of *jouissance* are made of pure emotion, which cannot be symbolized, nor translated, into words. When a psychoanalyst finds him or herself confronted with a patient having serious somatic trouble with essentially psychological causes, the analyst feels powerless before the opacity of a suffering that is irreducible. For this reason, my hypothesis of the Formations of *jouissance* is an attempt to organize, in a single category, the different pathological manifestations characterized by the massive eruption of this petrified emotion that Lacan had called "*jouissance.*" I have elaborated on the common traits of all of these formations in several texts in order to better understand and define the best therapeutic approach to treating the symptoms most resistant to analysis effectively.

My third thesis, often taken up by clinicians caring for patients for whom the symptoms are intermediaries between psychosis and neurosis, is that of "*local Foreclosure.*" It is a concept derived from a clinical observation that any practitioner can make. Take for example a common psychotic disorder, a delirious outburst or a hallucination, that suddenly appears in neurotic patients. In spite of the gravity of the problem, they do not reveal a psychotic structure; and, vice versa, patients diagnosed as psychotic present, apart from a particular delirium, behavior that is completely normal. I am thinking of a young man with a painful history marked by suicide attempts, with delirious episodes and several hospitalizations, who nevertheless, was able to explain his history to me clearly and sensibly. This case, among others, brought me to consider that foreclosure, a principal mechanism at the origin of psychosis, is triggered in a well-defined psychic space and only disturbs a single facet of the subject's life.

Before pursuing this farther, would you explain more about foreclosure?

It is not easy, but this is a technical term that necessitates a lengthy discussion. Briefly, the word *foreclosure* is a juridical term, which was proposed by Lacan in order to name a psychic break that is at the origin of a psychotic state. In order to understand it, we should compare it to the more banal repression of the neurotic. Both of them, *repression* and *foreclosure,* are defenses, specifically designed to confront distressing facts in the case of repression, or traumatic shock in the case of foreclosure. To repress an anguishing fact is to forget it. It is the usual attitude we adopt to deaden the blows of life. For the future psychotic, to foreclose a traumatic shock signifies a definitive refusal, not wanting to know anything about or to suffer from the violence of the aggression. This is a radical refusal to admit the trauma and to feel its pain. Now, such an absolute rejection of reality costs the person dearly. It inevitably triggers a seismic shock that fractures the psyche. It differs from repression, which is a normal defense mechanism. Defense by foreclosure is so brutal that it provokes a cleavage in the ego. When a person forecloses an unbearable trauma, the mind goes blank, a kind of mental gap that disturbs the psychical system, and creates psychosis. The majority of psychotic symptoms, such as delirium, hallucinations, and even suicide, are the desperate attempts of the ego to bridge the gap caused by the violence of foreclosure. You see, the ego rips apart, for it is incapable of accepting the pain of trauma. *To repress* is to admit the awful situation and then to forget it, while *to foreclose* is to erase or destroy the trauma, to the point of becoming psychotic, albeit in particular instances. It is true that psychoanalytic and neuroscientific hypotheses regarding the origin of mental illness are numerous, but that of foreclosure—true psychical blindness—is, from my point of view, one of the most pertinent for resolving the enigma of psychosis and improving its treatment.

Why did you qualify it by calling it *local* foreclosure?
Before answering your question, I need to prepare the way with some prefatory remarks. I will postulate that each individual is a plurality of personalities, a multiplicity of subjective beings, healthy and sick, coexisting in a single person. As I said, we think we are "one" but in fact we are "many." Each of these personalities, or, each of these subjective states, is in itself an imaginary scene, which is in general unconscious, composed of at least two characters, and whose plot is organized around an intense emotion. As such, the global psyche of an individual can be conceived of as a multilayered system, a kind of *millefeuille*, the layers of which are stacked on top of each other. If I had to describe my mental space, I would say: *I am a plurality of fantasized scenes, for the most part normal and healthy, sometimes pathological, piled up and connected by an invisible thread that secures my unity.* This theory of the *layered subject* enables me to explain how a serious psychotic, for example, can preserve healthy regions of his or her psyche; or, how a perfectly normal person living his or her daily life can be circumstantially psychotic, or locally disturbed, when under the spell of a pathological fantasized scene. I am convinced that we all have a seed of insanity that does not affect our stability; a localized madness we ignore. It is not made manifest by extravagant or bizarre behavior, but in the discrete form of a behavior that is illogical, rigid, peremptory, and repetitive, which we consider, nevertheless, to be perfectly legitimate.

This demonstrates that foreclosure reaches only one of the layers, one part of the framework that forms the structure of the subject. The damaged part of the structure can then either lead to the total collapse of the person—and then we would be dealing with a psychosis—or it can also respect the equilibrium of the psychic structure—and then we are dealing with a healthy individual who is also delirious, in a subtle way, in a small corner of his or her life. Incidentally, this discrete delirium can sometimes take the form of a creative passion without which no great works would ever be accomplished.

Do you carry on the work of Freud and Lacan?

Yes, Freud, Lacan, and other masters that I have made my own. The progress of a researcher, whatever the subject, always results from the work of his or her predecessors and the influence of his or her time. Assuredly, there is no research except within a tradition. Thus, my work takes up the heritage of what was transmitted to me by my teachers. I often say that the transmission of a science or an art is a movement in three parts: acquire, forget, and recreate. It commences with the acquisition of knowledge taught by our elders, followed by the forgetting of it, and completed by the recreation of the same knowledge. To receive a transmission is never to repeat it identically, but to reinvent knowledge learned. Of course, this reinvention is the completion of an immense effort of conquest. We only inherit knowledge bitterly won. This is exactly the principle that guides the disciple that I am. Every time I must address a theoretical problem, I begin by submersing myself in a study of the elders, then I forget it, then I try to reconstitute the knowledge I assimilated. This is how very often I surprise myself by advancing new propositions. If there is some degree of originality, it happens only through study. My motto could be written: *Say well what has already been said and you will be surprised to have said something new.*

CHALLENGE YOURSELF!

I do not want us to conclude without having brought up a question that concerns all young people today, namely, that of hope.
Hope is the absolute confidence that I have for the future. It is in effect a waiting; waiting for an accomplishment of which I will be the actor. But it is of little importance if this accomplishment takes place

or not, what counts is to be mobilized by the promise of tomorrow, even if it was an illusion. Hope alone prevails. It does so because it is a superior force that gives meaning to the present. So it follows that if you have confidence in the future, you will have the good fortune and happiness of savoring the *here and now* of life. The equation is as follows: by projecting yourself outside of yourself you will better manage life's daily trials.

Freud and Lacan belonged to traditionally religious families, Jewish and Catholic respectively, yet they declared that they did not believe in God. What do you think of that?
According to the definition I have just proposed, Freud and Lacan are, properly speaking, men of faith, because in order to blaze their trail, they had to have a real drive, which only the desire to overcome can give. But be careful to note, success was never their intention. It was something beyond that. It was a spontaneous drive, an unshakeable enthusiasm to move things forward. They let themselves be moved, and carried by an irrepressible force that pushed them to challenge themselves. It is this very force, external and transcendent, that was their God.

What is your God?
The god of psychoanalysts! Insofar as it exists, it would carry the name of the unconscious, as it is that which determines our thoughts, dictates our choices, and awakens our passions. What is the unconscious if not the force that pushes us to be what we should be?

To conclude, what final words would you like to address to young people who are reading this?
My message can be captured in two words: effort and humility. Ideas that remain nothing but thought, sculpture that is never realized, the poem that stays in one's dreams, are worth little in the end. The translation of the ideas into words, the transformation of the stone into a statue, or the composition of a poem, are all the kinds of things that require effort. The effort is long and painful, and yet, after having accomplished it, one has the feeling that it is very precious, more precious still because of the work it took to create it. Thanks to the work, we have taken from ourselves more than we had to give, and we have lifted ourselves onto our own shoulders.

The experience of effort is, for me, so formative that I never hesitate to say to young people: *Challenge yourselves!* Even though working hard is not in fashion, the future belongs to those who commit themselves to hard work.

As for humility, I understand it in the sense of doing what needs to be done, of accomplishing to the best of your abilities the task that is in front of you. I would say that to have a chance of succeeding, one must concentrate all of his or her energy on the present action without thinking of future success, such that the sentence one writes, or the line one draws, should be, at the moment they are executed, the only work that matters. The work is only in the act, however ordinary it may be. So here is a maxim that can guide a young person involved in a project: *Create with passion, and in so doing, create yourself.*

NOTES

EDITORS' PREFATORY NOTE TO THE AMERICAN EDITION

1. Juan-David Nasio, *A Psychoanalyst on the Couch*, Trans. Stephanie Grace Schull (SUNY Press, 2012), hereafter cited as PC, followed by the page number.

HOW DOES A PSYCHOANALYST WORK?

1. Please note that the telling of a story, even the most faithful, is always a work of fiction, the fiction of the person who composes the story. This remark applies to Lea and all of the other cases I bring up in this book.

2. Marguerite Yourcenar, *Memoirs of Hadrian*, Trans. Grace Frick (New York: Farrar Straus Giroux, 1963), p. 33.

LOVE AND SEXUAL PLEASURE

1. Colette Willy, *La Vagabonde* (Paris: Societé d'Éditions Littéraires et Artistiques, 1910), p. 279.

2. Ernest Jones, *The Life and Work of Sigmund Freud Volume II: 1901–1919 Years of Maturity* (New York: Basic Books, Inc., 1955), p. 421.

3. Richard Krafft-Ebing, *Psychopathia Sexualis*, Trans. F.J. Rebman (Brooklyn: Physicians and Surgeons Book Co., 1932), p. 202.

4. Sigmund Freud, "The Taboo of Virginity," in *The Standard Edition of The Complete Psychological Works of Sigmund Freud, Volume XI*, Trans. James Strachey (London: The Hogarth Press and the Institute of Psychoanalysis, 1986), pp. 193–194.

5. *The Schoolgirl's Companion*, in *René Char Selected Poems*, Eds. Mary Ann Caws and Tina Jolas (New York: New Directions Books, 1992), 11.

HATE AND FRIENDSHIP

1. Jacques Lacan, *Le Séminaire de Jacques Lacan, Livre VIII, Le Transfert 1960–1961* (Paris: Éditions du Seuil, 1991), p. 147.

2. In "The Concept of Hate," to appear in volume two of *l'Enseignement de 7 concepts cruciaux de la psychanalyse*.

IN PRAISE OF HARD WORK

1. TN. See the English language version of Dr. Nasio's lecture, "The Concept of the Subject of the Unconscious," in David Pettigrew and François Raffoul, Eds., *Disseminating Lacan*, Trans. Boris Belay (Albany: SUNY Press, 1996).

2. Antonio R. Damasio, *Descartes' Error: Emotion, Reason, and the Human Brain* (New York: G.P. Putnam's Sons, 1994), pp. 102–103.

3. Sigmund Freud, "The Ego and the Id," in *The Standard Edition of The Complete Psychological Works of Sigmund Freud, Volume XIX*, Trans. James Strachey (London: The Hogarth Press and the Institute of Psycho-analysis, 1986), p. 14.

INDEX

Printed in Great Britain
by Amazon